PREFACE

There is nothing like Interest to get children to read well, to read widely, and to understand what they read. The stories in this book are specially selected to arouse, maintain, and satisfy the interest of the pupils. The short paragraphs of Interesting Facts have a direct bearing on the stories, either by subject or scene, and should help considerably in the change from **learning to read** to **reading to learn**. The Questions on both Stories and Facts are **in sequence** and demand not only that the pupils read carefully but also that they remember the salient points. The answers (oral or written) can be used as **a direct aid to Composition**. The Development Exercises endeavour to expand on certain statements in the matter read, and the questions are designed to give the pupils an opportunity to express their thoughts and knowledge, simply and accurately.

These Readers are complementary to " The New First Aid in English," and therefore needless repetition, in language study and correct usage, has been purposely avoided.

A. M.

ACKNOWLEDGMENTS

We value highly the permission to include copyright material and are happy to put on record our indebtedness for:—

THE TALE OF A TAIL, to Enid Blyton.

A TICK-TOCK TALE, to Stephen Southwold.

TWO CLEVER BIRDS, adapted from the June volume of The Calendar Readers, by permission of Messrs. Macmillan & Co. Ltd.

THE LIGHTHOUSE, by Marjorie Wilson, by permission of Messrs. Basil Blackwell & Mott Ltd., Oxford.

THE STOLEN CHILD, by W. B. Yeats by permission of Mr. M. B. Yeats and Macmillan & Co. Ltd.

BURIED TREASURE, adapted from "The Squirrels' Hoard," by Mrs. Carey Morris, by permission of Messrs. Blackie & Son Ltd.

THE SCARECROW, by Michael Franklin, to The Poetry Society (Incorporated).

LONE DOG, by Irene R. McLeod, by permission of Irene R. de Sèlincourt.

THE TWO BROTHERS, from "Stories to Tell," by Maud Lindsay and

GULLS TO THE RESCUE, from "The Gulls of Salt Lake," by Sara Cone Bryant, from "Stories to Tell Children," by permission of Messrs. George G. Harrap & Co. Ltd.

I LOVE TO WALK WITH MUMMY, by Inez K. Sibley, by permission of the authoress.

THE SPANISH NEEDLE, by Claude McKay, by permission of the author.

GOD IN A HURRICANE, by Nellie Olson, by permission of the author.

TO A SQUIRREL AT KYLE-NA-NO, by W. B. Yeats, by permission of Mr. M. B. Yeats and Macmillan & Co. Ltd.

CONTENTS

		PAGE
1.	THE TALE OF A TAIL	7
2.	LUCKY AND THE GIANTS	16
3.	*I LOVE TO WALK WITH MUMMY*, by Inez K. Sibley	28
4.	THE THREE MONKEYS	29
5.	A TICK-TOCK TALE	30
6.	*TO A SQUIRREL AT KYLE-NA-NO*, by W. B. Yeats	40
6.	*IN GLENCULLEN*, by John Millington Synge	40
7.	BURIED TREASURE	41
8.	ST. GEORGE OF ENGLAND	51
9.	*THE RIVER*, by Faith Sharman	56
10.	THE LADY WITH THE LAMP	57
11.	THE PONY EXPRESS	66
12.	THREE CHARMS	75
13.	THE BELL OF ATRI	76
14.	ST. ANDREW OF SCOTLAND	87
15.	*THE SEA*, by Cecily E. Pike	93
16.	A STRANGE WARNING	94
17.	THE BROWNIE	101
18.	*GOD IN A HURRICANE*, by Nellie Olson	111
19.	TWO CLEVER BIRDS	112
20.	ST. PATRICK OF IRELAND	121
21.	*THE LIGHTHOUSE*, by Marjorie Wilson	126
22.	THE TWO BROTHERS	127
23.	SILK	137
24.	*THE PEDLAR'S CARAVAN*, by W. B. Rands	141
25.	GULLS TO THE RESCUE	142
26.	ST. DAVID OF WALES	151
27.	*LONE DOG*, by Irene R. McLeod	155
28.	LEATHER	156
29.	WILLIAM TELL	159
30.	*THE SCARECROW*, by Michael Franklin	166
31.	A BRAVE BOY	167
32.	THE BROWN KING	176
33.	*THE STOLEN CHILD*, by W. B. Yeats	190
34.	EMBLEMS OF OUR NEIGHBOURS	192
35.	SAFETY FIRST	194
36.	*AN EASTERN PROVERB*	196

THE TALE OF A TAIL

THERE was once a small brown and white guinea-pig called Tuppy. He led quite a happy life in a hutch and was well looked after by his young master. One night, however, he escaped . . . and how pleased he was to be free!

"Now I'm out in the big world!" he said. "I can go wherever I like! What fine adventures I shall have!"

He ran across the garden and then suddenly bumped into something large and soft. It was Sally the cat, who was carefully watching a mouse-hole in a green grassy bank.

"Clumsy! Why don't you watch where you're going!" she hissed at Tuppy, at the same time swinging her long bushy tail about in anger.

"What a fine tail!" exclaimed Tuppy, when he had recovered from his sudden fright. He tried to wave his own tail but couldn't . . . because he didn't have one.

Sally the cat looked at him and laughed. "My goodness! You've come out without your tail!" she said. "I shouldn't feel dressed without mine! What on earth have you done with it?"

"I don't know," said Tuppy, looking puzzled and searching the ground all around. "I must have dropped it somewhere."

"Well, here's Prickles the hedgehog. We'll ask him if he's seen it anywhere," said Sally with a wide grin. "Hi! Prickles! This poor little guinea-pig has lost his tail. Have you seen it anywhere?"

"I have just passed a bit of old rag in the ditch," said Prickles. "Would that be his tail?"

"Of course not!" cried Tuppy angrily. "Don't be so stupid!"

"Well, what is your tail like, then?" asked the hedgehog in a serious voice.

"I don't know," answered Tuppy. "I never noticed it till Sally told me that I must have lost it."

"Here's Jinks the brownie," said Sally, blinking at a little dark figure peeping out of the hedge. "Hi! Jinks! Have you seen Tuppy's tail? It's disappeared and we don't know where to find it."

THE TALE OF A TAIL

"Dear me!" said Jinks, with a sly wink to Sally. "Now let me see ... yes ... I did see a tail somewhere. I'll fetch it! I expect it belongs to Tuppy!"

Off he ran, and soon returned with ... what do you think ... a piece of string! "Here it is!" he cried with delight. "Your worries are over. I'll put it on again for you, Tuppy, and I'll make sure you won't lose it a second time."

"That's not *my* tail," said Tuppy, looking at the old bit of string in disgust.

"Well, if you don't know what your tail is like, how do you know that it isn't yours?" asked Sally. "Of course it's yours! Prickles! Give Jinks one of your spines to use as a needle. He can make a tiny hole in it for an eye, and then thread it with a long thin blade of grass. The tail can be sewn on very quickly and easily."

"He shan't! I won't let him!" cried poor Tuppy in alarm. "That isn't my tail . . . and it will hurt me dreadfully to have it sewn on. I'm going back at once to my nice comfortable home. I hate this adventure!"

With these words he fled . . . and how the other three naughty creatures laughed! Tuppy soon reached the door of his hutch and jumped quickly inside. He pushed the door with his nose until it clicked shut. At last he was safe and free from his tormentors. No more escapes for him, and he would try hard to forget about his lost tail.

Sally, who always delighted in teasing, wouldn't let him forget. Every time the tabby-cat saw him, she would approach the hutch and say, "Have you not found your tail yet, Tuppy? Too bad! What a pity! Now what could you have done with it?"

Poor Tuppy would pretend he was deaf and make no reply.

Enid Blyton.

THE TALE OF A TAIL

INTERESTING FACTS ABOUT TAILS.

Most animals have been provided by nature with the kinds of tails best suited to their ways of living, and the following animals show the different uses to which tails are put.

1. The **Cow** has a long tail with a small bush at the end, and this helps the creature to flick away the flies which worry it in the summer-time.

2. The **Horse** finds its bushy tail very useful as it is constantly fly-chasing in hot weather.

3. The busy little **Beaver** makes good use of his flat powerful tail when he is building, and his tail also acts as a paddle when he is swimming.

4. The quick **Monkey** has a long thin tail which it uses as an extra hand when leaping from branch to branch.

5. The jumping **Kangaroo** has a long, thick, powerful tail which acts as a third leg when bounding along in huge hops, and it also helps to support the heavy body when the animal is sitting upright.

6. The **Squirrel** uses his tail like a plane in helping to guide his flight in very long and high jumps.

7. The long heavy tail of the **Crocodile** not only acts as a rudder when swimming but is a dangerous weapon of attack and defence.

8. A **Cat**, when walking along a high narrow ledge, uses its tail as a kind of balancing pole by switching it from side to side.

9. Certain kinds of desert **Sheep** and **Mice** have very fat tails which they use as a food storehouse in the same way as a camel uses its hump.

THE TALE OF A TAIL

10. The **Rabbit's** little white bob-tail, known as a *Scut*, is sometimes used as a warning signal to its companions when it is chased by an enemy, or used as a guide post by other rabbits following it to safety. This also can be said of the **Fox**, whose tail is called a *Brush*, and of the **Hare**, whose tail is named a *Fud*.

QUESTIONS ON THE STORY.

1. What is the title of the story?
2. Give the name of the little guinea-pig.
3. What colour was he?
4. Where did he live?
5. How did he meet Sally the cat?
6. What was she doing at the time?
7. What did Sally say to him?
8. How did the cat show her anger?
9. What did poor Tuppy try to do?
10. Why was it impossible?
11. Who was Prickles?
12. What was the brownie's name?
13. What was he doing when Sally saw him?
14. What kind of tail did Jinks fetch for Tuppy
15. How did Sally say it could be sewn on?
16. What did the frightened Tuppy do?
17. What did the other three naughty creatures do?
18. The guinea-pig tried hard to forget about his ....
19. What did Sally say to tease him?
20. Poor Tuppy pretended that he was ....

READER—C

QUESTIONS ON THE INTERESTING FACTS.

1. Describe a cow's tail.
2. What kind of tail has a horse?
3. What use does a beaver make of his tail?
4. How does a monkey make use of his tail?
5. How does the kangaroo's tail help him?
6. The squirrel uses his tail..................................
7. How does a crocodile make use of his tail?
8. For what does a cat make special use of his tail?
9. Which creatures use their tails to store food?
10. (a) What is the name given to a rabbit's tail?
    (b) What is a fox's tail called?
    (c) What is the name given to a hare's tail?

DEVELOPMENT EXERCISES

1. The following are animals but the letters in their names have been mixed up. Can you tell what they are?
   OGD, SAS, REHSO, ATC, SOMEU, MELCA, TOGA, PESEH.

2. The guinea-pig squeals and the cat purrs. What sounds do the following creatures make?
   - (a) The pig ....
   - (b) The dog ....
   - (c) The cock ....
   - (d) The duck ....
   - (e) The mouse ....
   - (f) The owl ....
   - (g) The wolf ....
   - (h) The donkey ....

3. Make a list of animals which have horns.

4. Here are eight words—prickly, spotted, tall, burrowing, gentle, blind, striped, tiny. Which of the following animals does each word describe—mole, leopard, lamb, zebra, hedgehog, mouse, giraffe, bat?

5. Man has tamed many animals to help him.
   Which animals help :—
   (a) by working for him, (b) by supplying him with food?

THE TALE OF A TAIL

6. Which creatures are said to be :—
   (a) slow, (b) fast, (c) clever, (d) stupid, (e) brave, (f) timid, (g) strong, (h) hard-working, (i) lazy ?

7. Which creatures may be said to be (a) weavers, (b) hunters, (c) fishermen, (d) miners, (e) woodcutters ?

8. Here are footprints of a human being, a hen, an elephant, a cow, a duck, a horse. Can you place them ?

LUCKY AND THE GIANTS

ONCE there was a man called Lucky. He was a very timid man, but he liked to pretend to himself, that he was the bravest man in the world. He was always boasting of the great deeds he could perform but, as you might guess, he never did anything really brave. When no one was about, he would pretend he was fighting wild beasts and giants, and of course, he imagined he killed them every time.

One day, while crossing a field, he swung his sword wildly about him, and was soon engaged in a desperate battle with three imaginary giants. He killed three flies!

"Well, they might have been giants," said Lucky to himself, "and if they had been, I would surely have slain them." When he arrived home he proudly engraved these words on his sword, "This is the Sword of Lucky, Slayer of Giants."

Next day he took his sword, tied a small bag of flour on his back, and set off on a long journey. After walking for many miles he grew very tired and began to search for a good place to rest. He discovered a fine spot under a large tree, but before lying down, he buried

16

LUCKY AND THE GIANTS

his little bag of flour in the ground, in case thieves would rob him while he was asleep. Soon after, he was in the land of dreams.

At dawn next morning, while he was still fast asleep, seven real giants chanced to pass that way. They saw the sleeping Lucky and read the writing on the sword which was by his side.

"Oh!" said one of the seven. "Here indeed is a mighty warrior. We must ask him to show us what great deeds he can perform."

The loud voice of the giant awakened Lucky, and he was terrified at the sight of the seven huge men. He did not let them see how frightened he was, and when he noticed they were friendly, he spoke quite boldly to them;

"Well! What do you wish?"

"We should like to see you perform some great deed," replied one of the giants.

"That you shall see this very minute," replied Lucky. "See! This is the kind of man I am. When I stamp my foot, the earth shakes."

He walked over to the spot where he had hidden his little bag of flour under the soil. He stamped and stamped on the flour until the giants were almost hidden in clouds of white dust.

The giants were greatly surprised, and very much impressed. They begged him to come and live with them, and promised him great wealth and happiness. Lucky decided that he would like to stay with them for a few weeks, so he followed the giants to their woodland home.

One day a huge rhinoceros came to the forest where the giants lived. The rhinoceros is a very large ugly animal with thick wrinkled hide and a sharp strong horn on its nose. This beast did so much damage that the giants set out to hunt and kill it. They asked Lucky to go with them and help to get rid of the savage monster. He was really much too afraid to go, but at the same time he could not very well refuse.

"I will follow you in a few minutes," said Lucky, "as I must first sharpen my sword."

As soon as the giants had gone, Lucky, instead of sharpening his sword, climbed up a near-by tree to hide.

Presently who should come by but the dreadful rhinoceros grunting and snapping angrily. It lay down for a rest under the very tree in which Lucky was hiding. Suddenly the giants appeared and gave a great shout when they saw the rhinoceros. Poor Lucky almost fainted with terror, let go his hold of the branch, and fell right on top of the rhinoceros.

Up jumped the beast and away he went at full speed. Lucky clung on with both hands to the creature's ears as he was jolted and bumped through the forest.

Hot on their heels followed the seven giants and, after much racing and chasing, they at last managed to kill the rhinoceros with their spears. Instead of thanking the giants for saving his life, Lucky pretended to be very angry with them.

"Have you no sense! Could you not see that I was trying to tame the animal?" he cried. "That beast would have been very useful to us. It was so big and strong, and just what we needed to pull our heavy loads for us."

The giants said nothing but stared in astonishment at the brave little man who had tried to tame such a savage animal as a wild rhinoceros. They were now quite sure he must be the bravest man in the world.

About a month after this strange adventure with the rhinoceros, a loud shouting was heard near the woodland. A tribe of savages were on the warpath and were seeking to kill the giants and their friends. The giants came to Lucky and asked him to lead them against the enemy, but he made the same excuse as before—that he must first sharpen his sword.

When the giants had departed Lucky trembled with fear. He was much too timid to lead them, yet he knew that he could not refuse to help them. After a few minutes, Lucky chose the quietest-looking horse he could find and followed on the trail of the giants.

All went well until the horse heard the sounds of fighting. At once the creature went wild with the frightful noise and raced off like the wind. Poor Lucky tried to stop the animal by clinging to a young tree, but the tree came up, roots and all, in his arms.

LUCKY AND THE GIANTS

Away sped the terrified horse into the thick of the fight. The tree, which Lucky carried, scattered the enemy right and left and soon the savages fled in terror from the battle.

It was some time before Lucky could manage to control the horse and return to his friends, but when he did so, the giants welcomed him with open arms. They led him back to their camp with songs of joy and praise, and there he dwelt as a hero for the rest of his life.

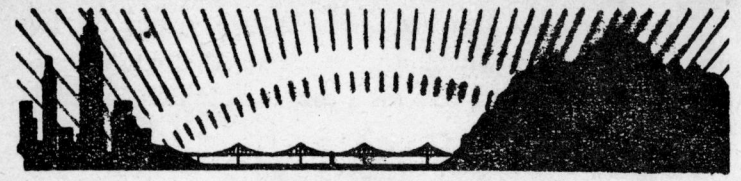

INTERESTING FACTS
ABOUT
GIANT THINGS
BIGGEST—HIGHEST—LONGEST

1. (a) The **highest mountain** in the world is Mount Everest between India and Tibet. It is over 29,000 feet high and was first climbed on 29th May, 1953, by a party of British climbers led by Colonel Hunt. The top was reached by a New Zealander, Edmund Hillary, and " Tiger " Tensing, a Sherpa native of Nepal.

   (b) The **longest river** in the world is the Nile in Africa.

2. (a) The **tallest office building** in the world is the **Sears Tower,** Chicago, 1,454 feet (443 metres), 110 storeys.

   (b) The **longest bridge span** in the world is the main span of the **Humber Estuary Bridge,** England, 4,626 feet (1,410 metres).

   The **longest cantilever bridge** in Great Britain is the **Forth Bridge,** Scotland.

   The world's **widest long span bridge** is the **Sydney Harbour Bridge,** Australia. The span is 1,650 feet (502 metres) and it is 160 feet (48 metres) wide.

LUCKY AND THE GIANTS

3. The longest and greatest **wall** in the world is **The Great Wall of China**, which is over 1,000 miles in length. It was built about 2,000 years ago to keep enemies from invading the country.

4. The greatest **caves** in the world are in **Kentucky** in the United States. They stretch underground for over 150 miles, and in them are rivers and lakes of black water, which contain fish without eyes.

5. The greatest **palace** in the world is the **Vatican**, which is the Pope's home in Rome.

6. The **biggest warship** in the world is the aircraft carrier **"Enterprise"**.

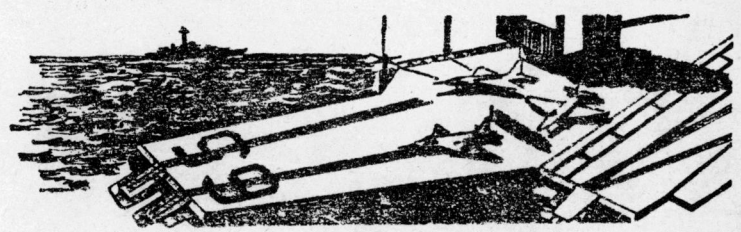

She is over 1,100 feet long, and over 250 feet wide.

7. The tallest **tree** in the world is the **sequoia or redwood** tree, which grows in the United States. This giant tree often reaches a height of 350 feet and has a trunk 35 feet thick.

8. The largest **creature** in the world is the **whale**. It lives in the seas near the North and South Poles but is not a fish. The largest **fish** is the **shark**.

9. The **largest animal** living on land is the **elephant** although it could be said that the **giraffe** is the **tallest**.

10. The largest **bird** in the world is the **ostrich**. It cannot fly but is a very fast runner. The largest **flying bird** is the **albatross**. It looks just like a huge seagull. The Albatross feeds on fish and is to be seen in the Southern Oceans. Measure 10 feet on the wall and you will have an idea of the wing span of this huge bird.

LUCKY AND THE GIANTS

QUESTIONS ON THE STORY.

1. What is the title of the story?
2. What words did Lucky put on his sword?
3. What did he take with him on his journey?
4. Where did he put it when he went to sleep?
5. Who chanced to pass while he was sleeping?
6. What did they ask Lucky to show them?
7. What did he do to impress them?
8. Where did Lucky decide to stay for a few weeks?
9. Why did the giants wish to kill the rhinoceros?
10. Where did Lucky hide?
11. How did he come to be on the monster's back?
12. What did Lucky say to the giants after they had killed the rhinoceros?
13. Who came to attack the giants?
14. What happened when Lucky's horse heard the sounds of fighting?
15. Describe how Lucky scattered the enemy in the battle.

QUESTIONS ON THE INTERESTING FACTS.

1. (a) Which is the highest mountain in the world?
   (b) Where is it?
   (c) Which is the longest river in the world?
   (d) Through which country does it run?
2. (a) Which is the highest building in the world?
   (b) In which city is it?
   (c) Which bridges may be said to be the greatest in the world?
   (d) In which countries are they?
3. (a) Name the greatest wall in the world?
   (b) How long is it?
   (c) Why was it built?

4. (a) Name the greatest cave in the world.
   (b) In which country is it?
   (c) How long is it?
   (d) What is strange about the fish which live in its waters?
5. (a) Which is the greatest palace in the world?
   (b) Where is it?
   (c) Who lives there?
6. (a) Name the biggest ship in the world.
   (b) Between which two places does it sail?
7. (a) Which is the tallest tree in the world?
   (b) How high does it grow?
   (c) How thick is its trunk?
8. (a) Name the largest creature in the world.
   (b) Where does it live?
   (c) Which is the largest fish?
9. (a) Which is the largest land-living animal in the world?
   (b) Which is the tallest animal?
10. (a) Which is the largest bird in the world?
    (b) What is strange about it?
    (c) Which is the largest flying bird in the world?
    (d) Where does it live?

DEVELOPMENT EXERCISES

1. The story could be called "Lucky and the *Seven* Giants."
   What number is missing in each of the following?
   (a) Cinderella and her .... ugly sisters.
   (b) Goldilocks and the .... bears.
   (c) Old King Cole and his fiddlers ....
   (d) Snow White and the .... dwarfs.
   (e) Ali Baba and the .... thieves.
2. The rhinoceros *grunted* angily.
        growls, screams, roars, bellows, barks, hisses.

LUCKY AND THE GIANTS

Which of these sounds do the following creatures make when they are angry? Use each word once only.
(1) The dog .... (2) The lion ....
(3) The bear .... (4) The bull ....
(5) The snake .... (6) The eagle ....

3. Put these creatures in order of size (smallest first).
   (a) rhinoceros, fox, mouse, elephant, rabbit.
   (b) hen, canary, ostrich, swan, parrot.
   (c) goldfish, shark, herring, tadpole, cod.

4. The story told of giants but the following are about little people. Who are they?
   (1) Little .... lost her sheep.
   (2) Little .... sat in a corner.
   (3) Little .... sat among the cinders.
   (4) Little .... sat on a tuffet.
   (5) Little .... went to visit her grandmother.

5. Put the following words in their right places in the sentence:—
   brave, timid, nervous, courageous, frightened, bold.
   Although Lucky was ...., ..., and ...., the giants thought he was ...., ..., and ....

6. A giant is a very tall man.
   What kind of man is a (a) hero, (b) miser, (c) bully, (d) coward, (e) dwarf, (f) glutton, (g) hermit?

7. In your village, town, or city, which is the
   (a) biggest shop, (b) highest building, (c) longest road, (d) biggest bridge, (e) oldest house?

8. Lucky had a sword and the giants used spears.
   What are the following?

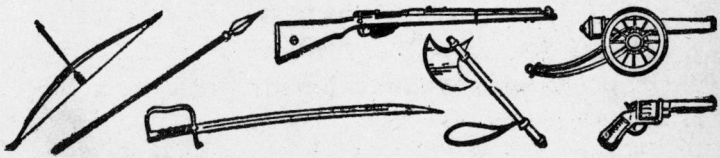

I LOVE TO WALK WITH MUMMY

I love to walk with Mummy, for she sees
　　Such lovely things: the poinciana trees
All blazing red, like Santa dressed to call
　　On little girls and boys, just one and all.

I love to walk with Mummy, for she sees
　　Such lovely things: a-nodding in the breeze
To us are bamboo plumes as we pass by,
　　They do not seem the very least bit shy!

I love to walk with Mummy, for she sees
　　Such lovely things: beneath the shady trees
A silvery fern, and gold, and many a flower
　　That make a perfect, perfect fairy bower.

And Mummy says she'll soon come tripping out,
　　I'd love to see her, so I'll wait about
'Side of this short cut, near the fairy gate.
　　I'm sure the Fairy Queen will not be late.
I love to walk with Mummy, for she sees
　　Such lovely things!

Inez K. Sibley

See No Evil—Hear No Evil—Speak No Evil.

THE THREE MONKEYS

In the land of Japan, far, far away,
There's a good little motto the people say,
" No evil see, though it appear;
No evil hear, though it be near;
No evil speak, no evil do;
See, hear, and speak what's pure and true."

AT Nikko, in distant Japan, there is a stable for the white pony of the god of the temple. Over the doorway is carved a group of three monkeys called the blind monkey, the deaf monkey, and the dumb monkey. The first monkey has his hands over his eyes, the second has his hands over his ears, and the third has his hands over his mouth. People say that they remind us not to look at bad things ; not to listen to bad things ; and not to say bad things. Many images of these monkeys have been made in metal or stone and sold in all parts of the world.

A TICK-TOCK TALE

" Hickory, dickory, dock,
The mouse ran up the clock ;
The clock struck one,
And down the mouse ran,
Hickory, dickory, dock."

"TICK-tock ! tick-tock ! " went the old grandfather clock in the hall ; " did I ever tell you the *true* story of Hickory, dickory, dock ? "

" You did not," said the barometer on the wall, " you never tell me anything except the time, and sometimes you are wrong."

" You cannot always be right," said the grandfather clock, rattling his weights with laughter ; " I have known you to say ' Very Fair ' when there was a thick fog outside."

" It was ' Very Fair ' somewhere else," replied the barometer crossly ; " but tell me your story."

" Well," went on the grandfather clock, " when I was very young, and even more handsome than I am now, I lived on a farm. I was the only clock for miles around, and so famous was I, that many people called at the farm just to see me. Even the children of the village would visit me and look up at my face and say, 'Oh yes, it's half past four.' Sometimes I would chuckle to myself because it was nothing of the kind."

"Now living on this farm was a sheep dog named Bob. He was a fine fellow and very good-natured. In fact he was too kind-hearted because he would lie dozing in his kennel and allow the mice to come and nibble the food under his very nose."

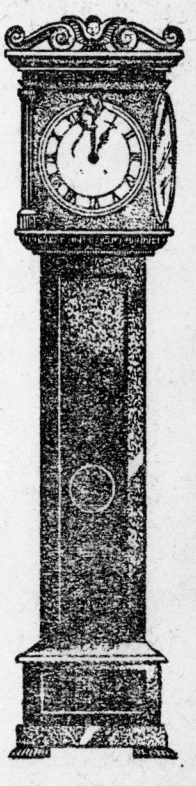

"One day Bob became sick, and could not do his work. Next day he was worse, and before a week had gone he was so ill that no one expected him to get better. One morning the farmer said to his wife, 'It will almost break my heart but I will need to shoot poor Bob. He is dying very slowly and very painfully, poor old chap. Call me in from work when the clock strikes one.' There were tears in the eyes of the farmers' wife but she said, 'Oh dear, I suppose it is the best way. Poor Bob has been suffering so much these last few days that I cannot bear to see him in such pain.'

"When the farmer had gone to the fields, his wife came over to me and wound me up. I think she must have been crying, because she forgot to fasten my face, and left it swinging open."

"Just as it was near one o'clock and I was getting

ready to strike the hour, a mouse came creeping through the open door, ran along the floor, up my body, and in the cheekiest way in the world, perched himself upon my big hand."

"Of course his weight made me stop at once and for the first time in my life I failed to do my duty and did not strike one."

"Because of this, the farmer's wife did not call her husband and he forgot all about his sad task till he came in for his supper in the evening. When he arrived and looked at Bob, he saw to his great surprise that the dog was wagging his tail."

"With a glad shout, the farmer turned to his wife and cried, 'Bless my soul, just look at Bob! He's wagging his tail to welcome me home! He must be getting better!' Better indeed he was, and in a few days the dog was romping about as happy as ever."

"No one ever knew what had made me stop. So you see," ended the grandfather clock with a giggle, "the old verse is wrong, because the clock did *not* strike one. It just shows you . . ."

"I don't want to know what it shows," snapped the barometer. "I think it is going to rain and I must attend to my duties."

Slowly and silently the pointer went round to "Rain."

From "*Tick-Tock*" *Tales, by Stephen Southwold.*

A TICK-TOCK TALE

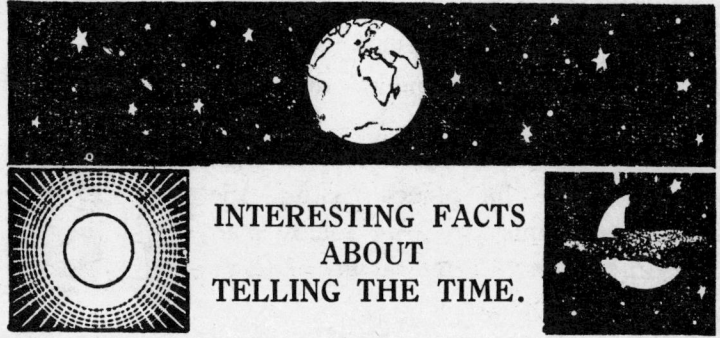

INTERESTING FACTS ABOUT TELLING THE TIME.

1. **The Sun.** People of very early times saw that the sun moved across the sky and from its position they could make a rough guess as to how much of the day had gone and how much of the day was still to come.

2. **The Moon.** In many countries, time was counted by the moon. It was not only seen that the moon moved across the night-sky but that it also changed its shape. Tribes, such as the Red Indians, used this method and spoke of "Many moons ago."

3. **The Shadow Stick.** In olden times people also noticed that as the sun rose higher in the sky so the shadows of things grew shorter. A stick was placed standing in the ground and they told the time of day by the length of the shadow.

33

4. The Sundial. The Sundial was invented from the Shadow Stick way of telling the time. This method depended not on the length of the shadow but on its direction. Marks and figures were made round the object casting the shadow and thus they were able to read the time of day. Sundials may still be seen in some gardens.

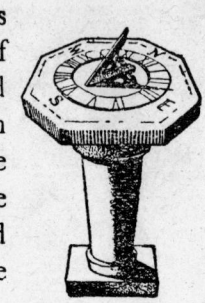

5. The Burning Rope. Another old way of telling the time was by means of a long burning rope which was knotted at even distances apart. The rope took the same time to burn between each knot and this gave some idea of how time was passing.

The Marked Candle. The marked candle was used in the same way as the burning rope. Marks were made at even distances on the candle and the owner could tell the time by the length of candle that had been burned.

6. The Sandglass. Some fine sand was placed in a special kind of bottle which had a very narrow neck in the middle. To measure time the bottle was turned so that the sand in the top part ran through the narrow opening into the bottom part. The

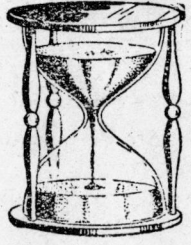

A TICK-TOCK TALE

most common one in use was the *Hour Glass*, in which the sand took an hour to pass from one part to the other. Nowadays, we use this method only in the *Egg-Timer*, a small three-minutes sandglass.

7. The Water Clock. The earliest kind of water clock was made by having two large tubs placed one above the other. The top tub was marked down the inside and there was a tiny hole in the bottom of it. This tub was filled with water and as it dripped into the other tub 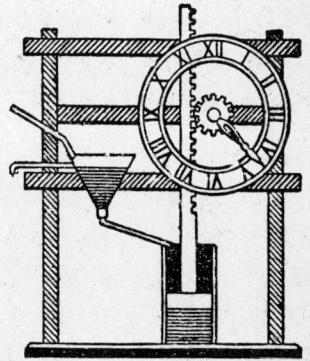 below, the time could be told by the marked levels of the water. This picture shows the first type of water clock with a hand.

8. The Pendulum Clock. This kind of clock worked by means of a steadily swinging weight fixed at the top to a cogwheel, which moved other cogwheels. The face or dial showed twelve hours marked in minutes and hours. There  were two hands—the longer one pointing the minutes and the shorter one pointing the hours. The earliest pendulum clocks were wound up by moving weights on a chain.

9. The Spring Clock. Present-day spring clocks and watches have generally two dials — the big face marked in minutes and hours, and the small face marked in seconds—so that three hands are needed. The hands move because springs force the cogwheels to turn. These clocks and watches are wound up by tightening a spring with a key or winding bar.

10. The Electric Clock. This kind of clock needs no winding as it has a wire to a plug and is kept going by electricity.

A TICK-TOCK TALE

QUESTIONS ON THE STORY.

1. What is the title of the story?
2. Give the verse of "Hickory, dickory, dock."
3. What kind of clock is telling the story?
4. Which two words describe the sound of the clock?
5. Where was the clock standing?
6. To whom did the clock tell the story?
7. Where was the barometer?
8. When very young, where did the clock live?
9. Who came to visit the clock?
10. What was the name of the sheepdog?
11. Why could he not do his work?
12. Why did the farmer say that he would need to shoot the dog?
13. When did he wish to be called in from work?
14. What did the farmer's wife do to the clock?
15. What did she forget to do?
16. At what time did the mouse appear?
17. Describe the actions of the mouse.
18. When did the farmer return from his work?
19. Why did he shout with joy?
20. Explain the difference between the verse and the story.

QUESTIONS ON THE INTERESTING FACTS.

1. How could the people of early times tell the time of day by looking at the sun?
2. Name any tribe which counted time by the moon.
3. Describe how time could be told by the Shadow Stick.
4. (a) Describe a sundial.
   (b) Where are sundials generally to be seen?
5. Describe :—
   (a) the burning rope way of telling the time.
   (b) the burning candle way of telling the time.

6. (a) How was time told by the sandglass?
   (b) For what purpose do we still use this method?
7. Describe the earliest kind of water-clock.
8. (a) Describe a pendulum clock.
   (b) What is a cogwheel?
9. If a spring clock or watch has two dials, how many hands are needed?
10. How is an electric clock kept going?

DEVELOPMENT EXERCISES

1. The farmer had a sheepdog.
   Name other animals likely to be seen on a farm.
2. " Hickory, dickory, dock,
   The mouse ran up the clock."
   Who (a) lost her sheep, (b) sat on the wall, (c) fell down the hill, (d) sat in a corner, (e) put the kettle on?
3. A clock tells us the time.
   What do the following tell us—watch, barometer, meter, thermometer, compass?
4. There are sixty minutes in one hour.
   How many minutes are there in (a) half-an-hour, (b) quarter-of-an-hour, (c) three-quarters-of-an-hour?
5. (a) Name as many different kinds of clock as you can.
   (b) Which kind of clock makes a noise to waken you?
   (c) Which kind of clock makes sounds every hour?
   (d) Sing the little tune which Big Ben plays just before it strikes the hour.
6. Draw seven little clocks just like those below and number them, 1, 2, 3, 4, 5, 6, 7.

A TICK-TOCK TALE

Put in the hands on each clock to show:—
   On clock 1—when you get up in the morning.
   On clock 2—when you have breakfast.
   On clock 3—when you go to school.
   On clock 4—when you have dinner.
   On clock 5—when you go home from school.
   On clock 6—when you have supper.
   On clock 7—when you go to bed.

7. (a) Give the short ways of writing the days of the week. The first one is done for you.
   Monday—Mon., Tuesday—............, Wednesday—............, Thursday—............, Friday—............, Saturday—............, Sunday—..........

   (b) Give the short ways of writing the following months of the year. The first one is done for you.
   January—Jan., February............, August............, September............, October............, November............, December............

8. Write out the dates of the year for:—
   (a) New Year's Day, (b) Christmas Day, (c) All-Fools' Day, (d) Independence Day, (e) your own birthday.

TO A SQUIRREL AT KYLE-NA-NO

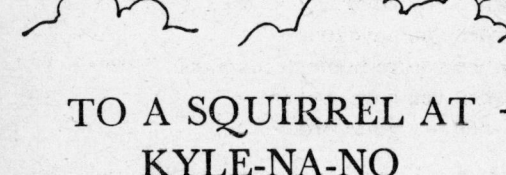

Come play with me;
Why should you run
Through the shaking tree
As though I'd a gun
To strike you dead?
When all I would do
Is to scratch your head
And let you go.

W. B. Yeats

IN GLENCULLEN

Thrush, linnet, stare, and wren,
Brown lark beside the sun,
Take thought of kestrel, sparrow-hawk,
Birdlime and roving gun.
You great-great-grandchildren
Of birds I've listened to,
I think I robbed your ancestors
When I was young as you.

John Millington Synge

BURIED TREASURE

WHEN we speak of buried treasure we think at once of gold and silver and diamonds hidden in the ground. This story will surprise you because it is not about any of these precious things.

Mr. Bushy Tail and his wife lived in a hole high up in a tall tree in the middle of a forest. They were such a happy little couple and had just set up house that spring. Now it was autumn and they were gathering together all the store of nuts they had been collecting for days. Never did you see two such busy creatures as they were . . running here and running there to carry the nuts one by one to a hole they had found at the foot of their house.

"Well!" said Mr. Bushy Tail with great pride, "You really are a helpful little wife. You've gathered as many nuts as I have. Now we need not fear the winter as we shall be quite well-off for food."

Mrs. Bushy Tail was too busy to reply but she waved her tail in pleasure and then set to work harder than ever.

Suddenly they heard footsteps coming towards them through the woods. The squirrels looked at each other in alarm and Mrs. Bushy Tail shot up the tree like a flash of lightning. Mr. Bushy Tail stayed behind for a moment or two in order to scatter some fallen leaves over the nuts in the hole, and then he too scampered quickly up the tree.

Alas, he was just that second too late to escape being seen.

"Oh! Look! A squirrel! See, Elsie, a squirrel . . . there . . . on that branch!"

"Oh, David, so it is! Why, there are two of them!"

For a few minutes they stood there talking and laughing and gazing up into the tree. Mr. and Mrs. Bushy Tail looked down and to their horror saw that at the foot of the tree, just in front of their little storehouse, stood a boy and a girl. Suddenly the boy noticed the little heap of leaves and bent down upon his knees.

"Look, Elsie! Look at what they have been doing!"

"Nuts!" said Elsie. "They were hiding them when we came long. They are watching us now to see what we will do!"

Two pairs of bright little eyes kept watching David as he picked up a nut from the hole, cracked it with his teeth, and began to munch.

"Try one, Elsie." The girl picked up a large nut, but suddenly dropped it again into the hole.

"David! It's not fair."

"Why not? We've found them and they don't belong to anybody."

"Yes, they do. They belong to the squirrels."

"But squirrels are not people."

"No, David! The squirrels have worked hard to gather these nuts, and it is their winter store. They are winter sleepers, and might starve to death if they cannot get food during the cold months. Think of what *we* should feel like if we lived in a hut in a wood and some great giant came along and stole all the food we had stored for the winter."

David dropped the second nut he was holding and looked a bit ashamed.

"It does seem rather mean," he said. "I didn't think of it like that."

"I'll tell you what we'll do," said Elsie. "Let's cover the nuts with the leaves again, and then hide behind a tree and see what happens."

"Right!" replied David.

Mr. Bushy Tail was trembling with fear and anger, and his little wife was almost in tears. To their astonishment, David and Elsie suddenly covered over the nuts with the leaves again and walked away.

How they scampered down the trunk and, with soft little noises of delight, finished the task of burying their treasure. From their hiding-place, David and Elsie watched and were glad.

"I'm so pleased we didn't rob their little bank," said David.

"Yes. So am I," replied Elsie. "They are safe now for the winter. Isn't it fun to know where their store is hidden? We can come and watch them digging up the nuts again."

Although they came back several times during the winter, they never saw the squirrels dig up their treasure.

Here is the reason.

Shortly after David and Elsie had gone home, Mr Bushy Tail said to his wife, "Those two giants will come back to annoy us again. I'm sure of it. We must move to another tree to-night. There is no time like the present."

BURIED TREASURE

In the light of the moon, the two little squirrels dug up all their winter hoard and moved it to a hollow tree in another part of the wood.

"There!" said Mr. Bushy Tail. "We have finished the job at last. Now we are safe. We can enjoy long sleeps during the winter, and when we waken now and then, our food will be fine and handy."

That is why David and Elsie never saw the squirrels again.

(Adapted)

INTERESTING FACTS ABOUT WINTER SLEEPERS.

1. The Squirrel

The little squirrel stores up food for the winter, makes himself a cosy bed in an old tree-trunk, and goes off to sleep. On warm days in winter, he wakes up, runs out to his store of nuts, has a good meal, and then returns to his bed for another long sleep.

2. The Hedgehog

As soon as winter comes, the hedgehog makes a cosy little nest among a pile of dead leaves and curls up inside it. He then goes into a very deep sleep and is difficult to waken during the cold season.

3. The Tortoise

At the first sign of winter, the tortoise finds a warm place and puts himself to sleep, not for the night, but for the whole winter. Every year he passes the cold months hiding and sleeping in some cosy spot.

BURIED TREASURE

4. The Badger
The badger passes a good deal of the winter asleep in his underground home, but now and again he has to go out and get food. After he has fed, he returns to his sett or lair and sleeps for weeks.

5. The Polar Bear and the Arctic Fox
In the cold and frozen places near the North Pole only the mother polar bear and the Arctic fox may be said to go for a long sleep in winter. The polar bear hides away under the snow but keeps open a little passage through which she can get air. The Arctic fox stores up food so that he can eat it when he wakes up now and again during the winter.

6. The Bat
Perhaps the soundest of all winter sleepers is the bat ; that horrid-looking mouse-with-wings creature which lives in the dusty corners of old buildings. At the end of autumn it may be seen hanging upside-down from the rafters and it remains quite still in this position till the cold weather has passed.

7. The Frog and the Toad

Frogs and toads sleep very soundly through even the coldest winter. Near the end of autumn they dive down to the bottom of the pond and bury themselves in the mud. Here they are safe and snug during the cold, foodless days of winter.

8. The Snail, the Slug, and the Worm

Snails, slugs, and worms are all sound winter sleepers. A snail not only sleeps in a hole in the ground but protects himself from the cold by making a thick cover to close the mouth of his shell. The slug makes a tiny nest in the earth and the worm always makes its winter home deep enough to escape the frost.

9. The Snake and the Lizard

Snakes and lizards hate cold weather. They hide away in some safe sheltered place, coil themselves and go to sleep during the months of winter.

10. Trees, Plants, and Flowers

Most trees, plants, and flowers may be said to sleep during winter. The weather is so cold and there is so little sunshine that they don't get a chance to grow. In spring, however, buds appear and everything comes to life again.

BURIED TREASURE

QUESTIONS ON THE STORY

1. What is the title of the story ?
2. What does buried treasure usually mean ?
3. What kind of animals were Mr. and Mrs. Bushy Tail ?
4. Why is this a good name for squirrels ?
5. Where did the squirrels live ?
6. When did they first set up house ?
7. In what season did the squirrels gather the nuts ?
8. Why did they collect them ?
9. Where did they store them ?
10. How did the squirrels hide the nuts ?
11. What did the little creatures hear coming towards them ?
12. What did Mrs. Bushy Tail do when she heard the noise ?
13. Why did Mr. Bushy Tail stay behind for a moment or two ?
14. What was the boy's name ?
15. What was the girl's name ?
16. Who first noticed the little store of nuts ?
17. What did he do with the nut he picked up ?
18. What did Elsie do with the nut ?
19. Why did she say that it wasn't fair ?
20. What happened after David and Elsie had gone home ?

QUESTIONS ON THE INTERESTING FACTS

1. Which countries have very cold winters ?
2. What does the hedgehog do in winter ?
3. How does the squirrel prepare for winter ?
4. How long does the tortoise sleep ?
5. Why is the Arctic fox like the squirrel ?
6. Which creature spends the winter hanging upside-down ?
7. Where do frogs and toads go in the winter ?
8. Why does the worm make a deep winter home ?
9. How do snakes and lizards spend the winter ?
10. Why do we say that trees, plants, and flowers sleep during winter ?

DEVELOPMENT EXERCISES

1. The squirrel has a covering of fur. What kind of covering has a (1) sheep, (2) starling, (3) rabbit, (4) fish, (5) dog, (6) hedgehog?

2. Place the following animals in order of size (smallest first):—deer, elephant, field-mouse, dog, cow, squirrel, horse.

3. The hedgehog, rabbit, and the field-mouse live in holes in the ground. Name other animals which have underground homes.

4. Some animals are bold and some are timid. Give the names of five bold fearless animals and five shy timid creatures.

5. The squirrel lives in a hole in a tree. His home is called a drey. Which kind of creature would you expect to find in a (1) stable, (2) nest, (3) sty, (4) hive, (5) byre, (6) coop, (7) burrow?

6. Name two animals which are good at (1) climbing, (2) digging, (3) running, (4) jumping, (5) swimming.

7. Many creatures find a warm place and go to sleep for the winter
    (a) Where do most birds go in winter?
    (b) Name three birds which stay all the year round.

8. Birds sometimes make their homes in strange places.
    Name a bird which makes its nest (a) in a bush or tree, (b) in the tops of high trees, (c) on the ground, (d) on the faces of cliffs at the sea, (e) on the tops of high mountains.

SAINT GEORGE OF ENGLAND

SAINT George is the special saint of England and the twenty-third of April is Saint George's Day. He lived a long time ago, and many stories are told about him. Once, when his journeys led him to the land of Egypt, he met with the following adventure.

One evening Saint George asked shelter for the night from an old hermit who lived in a small hut by the wayside.

"Certainly," replied the old man. "You are welcome to my humble home."

After taking off his armour and laying aside his famous sword and pure white shield on which was marked a blood-red cross, he noticed that the old hermit looked very worried.

"Why do you look so sad?" asked the young knight.

"I have good reason to be troubled," said the hermit. "Sad indeed is my story."

"In yonder town of Silene there is great sorrow, for, in the marsh nearby, dwells a terrible dragon. It has a body like that of a crocodile, but is covered with big brass scales. It has great wings as large as the sails of a ship. Its long tail can lash with such force that it could easily kill a man, and its claws are sharp and cruel. Worst of all, its savage jaws have teeth of iron, and from its nostrils come smoke and fire.

Soldiers have been sent to kill it, but they have always been driven back. Many different ways of destroying it have been tried, but all in vain.

Each day the terrible creature comes to the town, and each day two sheep have been sent out from the gates to feed the monster. These it has gobbled up greedily before returning to its lair in the marsh.

Matters have become worse because all the sheep and cattle have been eaten by the monster. The people of the town are now giving the dragon a person to eat each day."

" Let me rest a little," said Saint George.

" To-morrow you can show me where the dragon lives, and I shall fight the monster."

After breakfast next morning, the old hermit showed the young knight the way to the town of Silene. Towns in those days had a high wall right round them, with big gates where roads led into the town, so that once inside and the gates closed, the people were safe from their enemies.

As Saint George approached the town of sorrow, he saw one of the gates open, and a young maiden come out. She was alone and weeping bitterly. The unhappy girl had said farewell to her parents and was setting off to meet her death.

When he reached her, the young knight stopped his fine white horse and asked what was the matter.

"I am the King's only daughter," she answered, "and it is my turn to go to the marsh to be eaten by the dragon. You are in great danger! Go away at once or you will be killed too!"

"Fear not, gentle maid," said Saint George. "With the help of God, I shall slay the dragon and set your people free."

Quickly he lifted her on to his horse and took her to a place of safety. The young knight then turned towards the marsh and in the distance saw the dragon approaching. It was rushing towards him making a noise like thunder and breathing out clouds of smoke and fire.

Saint George charged at it but his spear glanced off the big brass scales. Again and again he struck but his blows did not seem to harm the creature. Suddenly the young hero and his horse were knocked to the ground by a lash from the monster's terrible tail. As the dragon raised itself over him, he drove his spear under one of its wings and seriously wounded it.

With a cry of rage and pain, the huge creature fell back and retreated a short distance. This gave Saint George time to jump up and get on horseback again. He discovered, to his dismay, that his spear was broken and so he was forced to use his sword.

The fight, however, was by no means over, as the dragon soon returned to the attack. For hours and hours they struggled until at last he managed to thrust his sword deep into the monster's mouth and it fell dead at his feet.

Not long afterwards the people of the town heard a great shout and, rushing to the watch-towers, they were amazed to see their Princess alive and well and by her side a handsome young knight.

At first the guards were afraid to open the gate but when Saint George cried, "The dragon is dead!" they went out to meet them with shouts of joy and gladness.

SAINT GEORGE OF ENGLAND

So ended the fight between Saint George and the dragon. If you look at the back of a Bank of England pound note you will see two pictures of the young knight about to kill the monster. Saint George had many other adventures, for he was always ready to protect the weak and the innocent.

(Adapted).

QUESTIONS ON THE STORY.

1. What is the title of the story?
2. In what country did the story take place?
3. Where did the old hermit live?
4. Describe the young knight's shield.
5. What was the name of the town of sorrow?
6. Describe the dragon.
7. Where did the monster live?
8. How did the people feed this terrible creature?
9. What happened when they had no more cattle or sheep?
10. How did people in towns protect themselves in those days?
11. As Saint George approached the town who came out?
12. What did she say to him?
13. What did he do?
14. What happened when Saint George charged the dragon?
15. How were the young hero and his horse knocked to the ground?
16. Where did he wound the monster?
17. What happened to his spear?
18. How did he kill the dragon?
19. Where will you see a picture of the fight?
20. Saint George always protected the .... and the ....

THE RIVER

This is the tale of a river so wide,
That grew from a streamlet upon a hillside,
It bubbled and gurgled and on its way leapt,
Right over a rock and then on it crept,
Between grassy banks, where it talked to the flowers,
Of warm friendly breezes, and soft summer showers,
It flowed through a meadow where cows came to drink,
And where weeping willows grew on its brink.
It came to a mill and turned the wheel round,
Which helped the good miller's fine wheat to be ground.
But soon that broad river swept round a big bend
And said to itself " Why this is the end,"
It seemed really pleased and it sparkled with glee,
As it poured its glad water right into the sea.

Faith Sharman.

THE LADY WITH THE LAMP

> " *A lady with a lamp shall stand*
> *In the great history of the land ;*
> *A noble type of good*
> *Heroic womanhood.*"

FLORENCE NIGHTINGALE was born in Italy in 1820 and she was named after the town of her birth. Her parents were British and their home was in a Derbyshire village. When quite a child she was kind and helpful to all in distress and she was very fond of the little creatures of the woods. The following story shows her kind nature.

Living near the village was a fine old shepherd named Roger, who had a splendid sheep-dog called Cap. Every day they could be seen out on the hills from early morning till dusk ; the shepherd carrying his long crook, and the dog following faithfully at his master's heels.

One day, as Florence and another girl were out walking, they noticed that the sheep were running in all directions and that old Roger was having a hard time trying to keep them together. By the look of things he wasn't managing very well and the two girls stopped to ask him what had become of his dog.

" Oh ! " replied the shepherd, " I really don't know what to do ! Cap will never be able to help me any more. I am sorry that the poor fellow will have to be destroyed."

" Destroyed ! " said Florence. " Do you mean that you must put an end to him ? How could you be so cruel ? Where is he now and what has he done ? "

" He has harmed nobody," replied Roger ; " but yesterday a cruel stupid boy threw a big stone at him and broke his right foreleg."

The old man spoke in a very sad voice and Florence was quite sure she noticed a tear in his eye.

" Poor Cap ! " said the shepherd. " He is as wise as a human being and such a true and faithful friend. He knew my every wish and was so obedient to my orders."

" Would you mind if we called to see him ? " asked Florence. " We might be able to do something for him."

" It is very kind of you," replied the shepherd. " He'll welcome you, I'm sure. He must be feeling rather lonely just now, as I have been out on the hills all day."

Florence and her friend went on to the shepherd's cottage and called in to see the poor dog. When the girls talked to him, he began to wag his tail. Then he crawled from under the table, and lay down at their feet. Florence took hold of one of his paws and patted his rough head while her friend looked at the injured leg.

It was badly swollen and it hurt him to have it touched ; but he licked her hands for he knew she was trying to help him.

"It's only a bad bruise. I'm glad to say there are no bones broken," said Florence's friend. "If Cap rests for a few days he should be well again."

"Thank goodness!" exclaimed Florence. "Can we do anything to ease his pain?"

"Yes. Bathe his leg with warm water. That should help."

Florence lit the fire, made ready some hot water, and began to bathe the poor dog's leg. It was not long before he tried to show his thanks by wagging his tail.

On their way back they met the old shepherd coming slowly homewards.

"Oh Roger!" cried Florence. "You will not lose poor old Cap after all. We have found that his leg is badly bruised but not broken."

"I am delighted to hear it," said the old man. "Many thanks for going to see him."

The next morning Florence rose early and went to bathe Cap's leg. The following day she bathed it again, and in two or three days the dog was as fit as ever and able to look after the sheep for his master.

Florence Nightingale was a young woman when war broke out between Britain and Russia. Most of the fighting took place in a part of Russia called Crimea. Hundreds of soldiers were killed or wounded, and many others died from sickness, cold or famine.

It was at this time that she made up her mind to help the weak and suffering soldiers and she sailed with a band of nurses to Crimea. Everything was in a terrible mess when they arrived.

They started by making the hospitals as clean as possible. Windows were opened to let in fresh air. Food was well cooked and beds were kept clean and tidy. Everybody was eager to help her in her fight against dirt and disease.

Night after night, when her hard day's work was done, she passed from room to room with a lantern in her hand. She spoke a few kind words to one, smoothed the pillow of another, and tried to get them to sleep soundly and well. Soon she was called by the soldiers " The Lady with the Lamp."

As she could scarcely find time to rest from her work, she became very ill. Luckily she got well again and was able to go back to help her brave nurses.

When Florence Nightingale returned to this country she did a great deal to improve our hospitals. Her life was spent in helping the sick and the poor and she received high praise from many lands for her noble work.

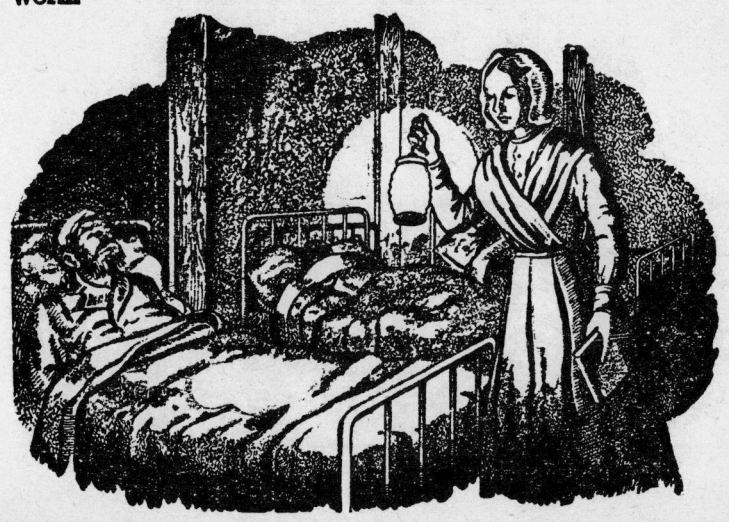

10 READER—C

INTERESTING PICTURES
ABOUT
PEOPLE IN UNIFORM
WHO GIVE PUBLIC SERVICE

THE LADY WITH THE LAMP

QUESTIONS ON THE STORY.

1. What is the title of the story?
2. Where was Florence Nightingale born?
3. What was the old shepherd's name?
4. What was the dog called?
5. One day Florence and another girl were out ....
6. Why did they stop to speak to the shepherd?
7. Why were the sheep running in all directions?
8. What did the shepherd say was the matter?
9. Where did Florence and her friend go?
10. What was wrong with Cap?
11. How did Florence help to ease the pain?
12. In what way did Cap show his thanks?
13. What happened as a result of her care and kindness?
14. War broke out between .... and ....
15. Where did most of the fighting take place?
16. What did Florence make up her mind to do?
17. How did she make better hospitals?
18. Why did the soldiers call her "The Lady with the Lamp"?
19. Why did she become very ill?
20. What did she do when she returned to this country?

QUESTIONS ON THE INTERESTING PICTURES.

1. (a) What does a nurse do?
   (b) Describe her uniform.
2. (a) How does a policeman help us in many ways?
   (b) Why are bad people afraid of him?
3. (a) A postman delivers .... and .... to your home.
   (b) What colour is a pillar-box?
4. (a) Why does the fireman wear a helmet?
   (b) Why does he wear high leather boots?
5. (a) What does a bus conductress give you when you pay your fare?
   (b) How does she signal "stop" and "start" to the driver?

6. (a) Where is a porter to be seen ?
   (b) What is his work ?
7. (a) How would you know an ambulance ?
   (b) Where does it take injured people ?
8. (a) Where does a lifeguard stay ?
   (b) What does he do when he sees a swimmer in distress ?
9. (a) What is the first duty of a lighthouse keeper ?
   (b) Why is it usually a lonely life ?
10. (a) A lifeboatman is a very brave man. Why ?
    (b) What does he wear ?

DEVELOPMENT EXERCISES

1. What am I called ?
   (a) I dig coal.
   (b) I cut boys' hair.
   (c) I draw and paint pictures.
   (d) I make men's suits.
   (e) I mend burst pipes.
2. Who sells (a) bread and cakes, (b) mutton and beef, (c) sugar and flour, (d) fish, (e) apples and bananas ?
3. A nurse uses *scissors and bandages*.
   Who uses (a) safety-lamp and pick, (b) anvil and hammer, (c) weights and scales, (d) plough and tractor, (e) saw and plane ?
4. Cap was a sheep-dog who worked for his master.
   Which of these animals have been tamed to work for man :— tiger, camel, giraffe, horse, lion, fox, ox, donkey, elephant, panther ?
5. The shepherd looked after his flock on the hills.
   Name two people who work (a) in the open air, (b) in factories, (c) in shops, (d) in ships, (e) in railway stations.

THE LADY WITH THE LAMP

6. Cap's *foreleg* was badly bruised.
   What do we call?
   (*a*) the part joining the head and the body.
   (*b*) the middle joint of the leg.
   (*c*) the middle joint of the arm.
   (*d*) the joints between the hand and the fingers.
   (*e*) the long bone down the middle of the back.

7. *Nightingale* is also the name of a bird.
   (*a*) Give two other names of birds which are used as names for people.
   (*b*) Give two names of animals which are used as names for people.

8. Make signs with face and hands to show that you are (*a*) tired, (*b*) thirsty, (*c*) angry, (*d*) sleepy, (*e*) frightened, (*f*) happy, (*g*) sad, (*h*) proud.

THE PONY EXPRESS

THE first settlers who went to America lived along the coast and did not go far from the sea because of the great forests and high mountains which barred their way. After a time, however, some brave hunters and fur traders began to travel beyond the forests and mountains. Quite often they returned with wonderful stories about the rich land and wild animals they had seen.

It was not long before many families made up their minds to go together to this wonderful land that lay on the other side of the mountains. It was a very dangerous journey as they had to fight against Red Indians and bands of robbers. When they found a good place to make their homes, they joined together to build log cabins for each other. In this way, little villages and towns sprang up all over the country.

As people were eager to hear news of their friends, men were hired to carry letters from one place to another. These postmen did not start out until they had gathered enough letters to pay for the trip. People complained about them as they sometimes took months to deliver a letter.

THE PONY EXPRESS 11

Stage coaches were next used to carry passengers, goods, and mail between the towns. Even this way was too slow for important letters and messages. To meet the wishes of the people for a speedy and safe delivery of letters, the Pony Express was started.

A company bought five hundred swift strong ponies, and built a chain of offices and stables between the East and the West. They also hired eighty of the best horsemen in the country.

These pony riders had to be brave, clever, and cool in times of danger. Each rider had his own run and had to cover the distance between two stations which were usually about fifty miles apart. They changed their horses every fifteen miles and they made no stop to eat or rest until they reached the end of their journey.

The letters were wrapped in oiled silk because the express rider had sometimes to swim streams in order to avoid danger. He carried these silk-covered bundles in two small leather pouches strapped to the saddle.

These brave riders faced many hardships and dangers. No matter how cold or stormy the weather, they had to be ready to leap into the saddle and dash forward to the next station. They had to find their way over lonely and dangerous trails. Often bands of Red Indians or robbers would attack them and they would narrowly escape with their lives.

The best known of the Pony Express riders was William F. Cody, who became the famous " Buffalo Bill." He had to seek work when he was fourteen years of age because of his father's death.

One day young Cody met a man who was helping to start the Pony Express Company.

"Cody," said the man, "we are starting the Pony Express in a very dangerous part of the country. It will be hard and exciting work, and we are looking for only the best and most fearless riders. Will you take the job?"

As the pay was very good and he had his mother and young brothers and sisters to support, Cody answered at once, " Thanks. I'll be glad to start work right away."

It was not long until Cody made the longest Pony Express ride on record. After a trip of more than a hundred miles he reached the station only to find that the next rider had been killed by Red Indians. There was

THE PONY EXPRESS

no one to go on with the mail and this brave lad felt that it was his duty to do so. He changed ponies and was off on another long dangerous ride.

Cody nearly lost his life on this part of the journey. Shortly after leaving the station he was ambushed by a band of Redskins on the warpath. They surrounded him but he escaped by suddenly lying flat on his horse and charging through them. There was a long and exciting chase but he managed to avoid capture.

When he arrived at the next station, Cody discovered that he must return at once with a very important message. Off he went again by the same way as he had come and, although he was very tired and weary, the mail was delivered on time. In all, he had ridden about three hundred miles with stops only to change to fresh ponies.

With the coming of the railway and the telegraph, the Pony Express stopped, as it was no longer needed. William Cody soon found a job with the railway company. He hunted and killed buffaloes in order to supply meat to the men who were building the railway. That was how he came to be called " Buffalo Bill."

INTERESTING FACTS ABOUT SENDING MESSAGES

1. Long, long ago, messages were carried from one place to another by **men on foot**. At one time in Scotland, when news of danger was received, a small wooden cross was made, set alight, and carried by runners from village to village.

2. Another old way of sending messages was to light fires on the tops of certain high hills. These **beacons** formed a chain through the country and the news of danger spread very quickly.

3. In order to get letters delivered much more quickly and safely, **men on horseback** were used instead of runners.

4. When a regular service was started, letters and goods were sent by **mail-coach**. Sometimes the coach had to be guarded against robbers and highwaymen.

5. Red Indians used to send messages by means of **smoke signals**. This was done by waving a large skin over a smoking fire. African tribes sent messages by playing on big drums called " **tom-toms.**"

6. Messages were sometimes sent by **carrier-pigeons**. These birds, when set off, returned to their home lofts with the notes tied to their legs.

THE PONY EXPRESS

Near the battle-front in war-time, **dogs were** often used to carry special messages.

7. Sending messages by **flags** in daylight, and **light flashes** when dark, were commonly used by the army and navy. The alphabet of dots and dashes was called the " Morse Code," and the alphabet where two flags were used in daylight was called " Semaphore."

8. The **telephone** is a very quick and handy **way of** speaking to some one who is some distance away.

9. **Wireless** and **television** are now used a great **deal** to give news and entertainment in the home.

10. The **postal service** for letters and parcels is very quick, safe, and cheap. Here are the various stages :—

Stamped letter put in pillar box—collected by postman in van and taken to sorting office—address read by sorter and letter put along with others to be sent to the same place—carried in special bags by motor, train, steamer, or plane to the nearest sorting office to the address on the letter—delivered to house by postman.

QUESTIONS ON THE STORY.

1. What is the title of the story ?
2. Where did the story take place ?
3. Where did the first settlers live ?
4. Why was it dangerous to go beyond the forests and mountains ?
5. Why did the people complain about the first kind of postmen ?
6. What were next used to carry passengers, goods, and mail ?
7. How many ponies did the Express Company buy ?
8. How many horsemen did they hire ?

11   READER—C

9. How far apart were the stations?
10. The riders changed their horses every .... **miles.**
11. How did the express riders carry the letters?
12. Who was the most famous of the Pony Express riders?
13. At what age did he start work?
14. Why had he to begin work so young?
15. One day Cody reached the station to find ....
16. What did he do?
17. How did he escape from the Redskins?
18. Why did the Pony Express stop altogether?
19. Where did William Cody find his next job?
20. Why was he called " Buffalo Bill "?

QUESTIONS ON THE INTERESTING FACTS.

1. (a) How were messages sent in olden times?
   (b) What was the " Fiery Cross "?
2. Where were beacons lit to pass on messages of danger?
3. What later took the place of messengers on foot?
4. When a regular service was started, how were letters and goods sent?
5. (a) How did Red Indians sometimes send messages?
   (b) How do some African tribes send messages?
6. (a) How do pigeons carry messages?
   (b) Which creature was sometimes used to carry messages in war-time?
7. (a) How do the army and navy send messages (1) in day-time, (2) at night-time?
   (b) What name is given to the alphabet of dots and dashes?
8. What is a very quick and handy way of speaking to a person who is some distance away?
9. What are now used to give news and entertainment in the home?
10. What happens when you post a letter?

CAN YOU NAME THEM?

DEVELOPMENT EXERCISES

1. The pictures at the side of this page give a story without words. Can you tell it?

2. Give the plural of:—knife, story, tooth, sheep, thief, buffalo, child, postman, deer, valley.

3. A pony sleeps in a stable.
   Which animals sleep in a (1) sty, (2) kennel, (3) burrow, (4) pen, (5) earth?

4. The rider was attacked by a band of robbers.
   What name is given to a number of:—sheep, cattle, trees, thieves, wolves?

5. Name four different ways in which mail can be carried from one place to another.

6. What is the postage on a letter?

7. Name four different ways of sending messages nowadays.

8. A pony is not a young horse. It is a special kind of small horse.
   (*a*) What is the long hair on a pony's neck called?
   (*b*) Of what use is a saddle?
   (*c*) How is a pony guided?
   (*d*) Why are iron shoes put on the hooves?
   (*e*) What is a bit?

THREE CHARMS

I

IN the morning when ye rise
    Wash your hands and cleanse your eyes;
Next, be sure ye have a care
To disperse the water far;
For as far as it doth light,
So far keeps the evil sprite.

II

If ye will with Mab find grace,
Set each platter in his place;
Rake the fire up, and get
Water in ere sun be set.
Wash your pails, and cleanse your dairies:
Sluts are loathsome to the fairies.
Sweep your house—who doth not so,
Mab will pinch her by the toe.

III

If ye fear to be affrighted
When ye are by chance benighted,
In your pocket for a trust,
Carry nothing but a crust;
For the holy piece of bread
Charms the danger and the dread.

HERRICK
(1591-1674)

The word "charm" comes from a Latin word *carmen* meaning "a song". Charms are little verses, or single lines, or even single words, that are supposed to have magic in them against the powers of evil. Long ago there were charms to cure toothache and fevers and squinting, for such misfortunes were supposed to be the work of evil spirits. To-day some people still seem to believe in charms, lucky words and lucky symbols—horseshoes, wishbones, and the like. But four hundred years ago, when Herrick wrote, such beliefs were much stronger and his poems would be read seriously by everyone. Mab was the Queen of the Fairies and was sometimes drawn in a carriage by a team of tiny horses.

THE BELL OF ATRI

IN Atri, a town in Italy, there lived long ago a very rich man, who was Governor of the town. He was loved by all the people of Atri, not because he was rich, but because his heart was kind and true.

Now many of the people were poor, and times were often hard. Sometimes the crop failed and they had very little food to eat. The mothers and fathers grew sick and thin, and even the plates of the children were often empty.

The good Governor of Atri thought a great deal about the troubles of his people, and when they suffered hardship and hunger, his heart was moved to great pity. He built a little tower just outside his castle, and in the tower he put a bell from which a long rope hung almost to the ground.

The Governor made it known to the people that any person who was in trouble, sick, or hungry, need only ring the bell and help would be given at once. For many years the hungry came and rang the bell and were fed; the sick rang and were healed; the unhappy rang and were comforted. The rope was pulled so often that the end of it frayed, and the keeper of the belfry tied up the loose threads with bits of straw.

Then everything changed. Better times came to Atri; the harvests were good; the people prospered; and soon, in all that fair town, there was no one who was hungry, sick, or needy. The rope still hung from the bell but no hand came to pull it.

Now it so happened that at this time there lived in Atri a rich merchant whose business it was to carry goods from one part of the town to another. For many years his good horse Benito carried the heavy loads. Then it grew old and weak and half-blind and could not do the hard work that it had once done so easily. The merchant bought a young strong horse and then, very cruelly, turned poor old Benito out to shift for himself.

The old horse wandered sadly about the streets of Atri, peering with its dim eyes in search of something to eat. The days went by, and thinner and thinner and weaker and weaker grew Benito, for there was little food to be found, and no one thought to feed a useless old animal.

One evening, Benito limped slowly along the road to the Governor's castle. He reached the belfry and, seeing the straw at the end of the rope, began to eat it. Tug, tug, tug, went the worn old teeth of Benito and inside the tower the bell began to peal.

The Governor, who was at supper, heard it and summoned the keeper of the bell. " Go and see what is the matter," he said. " It is a long time since the bell has been rung for help."

When the keeper went down to the belfry he saw an old lame, thin, half-blind horse tugging at the bell-rope. He hurried back to the Governor and said, " There's no one there, sir ; just an old starved horse."

" No one ! " cried the Governor. " Is not a horse deserving of all the aid we can give ? Never shall the bell of Atri be rung and no help be given ! "

The Governor hastened to the belfry and, when he saw the horse, his eyes filled with tears. Then a gentle smile played about his mouth as he went up to Benito and patted his head.

" Well, Old Faithful !" he said. " You seem to be in need of food and shelter. Follow me and we will see what we can do for you."

Benito was led into the stables and there he was cleaned and fed. For the rest of his days Benito lived

THE BELL OF ATRI

happily with the Governor. The old horse did a little light work now and again, but he spent most of his time grazing in grassy meadows. Certainly he never again had to fear hunger or cold.

INTERESTING FACTS
ABOUT
THE CARE OF PETS

All boys and girls are fond of pets. If treated kindly, these creatures become very friendly and give you much happiness. No decent boy or girl would ever make them angry or be cruel to them.

1. A Pony should be fed on hay and oats four times a day and should be given water as often as he requires it. He also needs plenty of exercise and should have a nice clean stable. Always speak quietly to a pony before patting him. If you want to make friends with a pony, give him a carrot or some lump sugar, but remember to keep your hand and fingers flat. Don't shout suddenly at him and never strike him on the head. To clean a pony, rub him down with warm soapy water and then brush him dry.

2. A Dog is perhaps the most friendly of all pets. No animal is more faithful and no pet will put so much trust in you. He needs at least two good meals a day and enjoys a bone. Don't have him around the dining table to beg and eat scraps of food. Never interfere with him when he is eating or drinking. Train him in good habits when he is a puppy. A dog needs exercise and should have a cosy sleeping place which he knows is his own. Never keep him chained up for long and always see that he has a collar with his name and address on it. To clean a dog, wash him with warm soapy water and then brush him dry.

3. **A Cat** is a very proud creature although she likes to be stroked and petted. Feed her twice a day and see that she gets plenty of milk and fish. Train her in good habits when she is a kitten. Give her a warm cosy place of her own near the fire and keep her indoors at night. Many cats are left to wander about the streets and must often be cold and hungry. Be sure that she always wears a collar with her name and address on it. She will keep herself clean by licking her coat with her tongue.

4. **A Rabbit** makes an interesting pet and should be looked after very carefully. He needs a good clean home (hutch) and must get a little ground in which he

can run about safely. Feed him at least twice a day, morning and evening, on such foods as oats, bran, greens, and vegetables. To clean a rabbit, rub him down with warm soapy water and then brush him dry. Lift a rabbit with both hands and never hold him by the ears.

5. A Tortoise is another pet which needs great care. Keep him in a wired corner of the garden and let him have a box for shelter. Be sure that he has a warm cosy place to sleep in winter. The best plan is to dig a little burrow where he can bury himself in cold weather. Feed him on grass, dandelions, buttercups, cabbage, and lettuce. Never keep him in the one little spot by tying his leg to a post.

6. A Parrot is perhaps the most amusing pet of all, as he can be taught to talk and to sing songs. This bird needs a large cage which should be kept as clean as possible. If he is very tame and friendly you can allow him to move freely about the room. Feed him

THE BELL OF ATRI

on food which you can buy at a pet shop and remember to cover the cage with a cloth at night.

7. A Canary is a delightful little bird to keep as a pet. Give him a big roomy cage so that he can fly and hop about easily from spar to spar. Feed him on birdseed and change his drinking water every day. See that he gets a bath now and again and give him a bit of cuttlefish on which to sharpen and clean his beak. Keep the cage in a warm place away from the window and sprinkle the floor of it with sand. Cover his cage with a cloth at night.

8. A Budgerigar (sometimes called a "Budgie") makes a perfect pet as he is very tame and easy to keep. This gay little bird can be taught to sit on your shoulder, to eat out of your hand, and to talk just like a parrot. Feed him on birdseed and lettuce, and change his drinking water every day. See that he always has a nice clean cage and hang up one or two little bells with which he can play. Cover his cage with a cloth at night.

9. A Goldfish is a very good pet but he should never be kept alone. It is best to keep two or three of them in a large glass tank with fresh water, some sand, and small weeds. Feed them on bread crumbs, small worms, and insects, but good food for goldfish can be bought at any pet shop. See that there is no danger to the fish from cats.

10. A Minnow is a pet which has been kept at one time or another by almost every boy and girl. Like the goldfish, he should never be kept alone. Minnows

are found in ponds and are caught with little hand-nets. Keep them in a glass tank with fresh water, sand, weeds, and a few little stones. They will not live long in a small glass jam-jar. Feed them on small worms, insects, and food which you can buy at a pet shop.

QUESTIONS ON THE STORY.

1. What is the title of the story?
2. Where did the story take place?
3. Why was the Governor loved by all the people?
4. Why had they sometimes little food to eat?
5. What did the Governor build just outside the castle?
6. What was in the tower?
7. What did the Governor tell the people?
8. The rope was pulled so often that the end of it ....
9. How did the keeper repair it?
10. In what ways did things change for the people?
11. What kind of business had the merchant?
12. What did he need for his business?
13. What was the old horse's name?
14. Why was the poor animal turned out of his stable?
15. What was Benito forced to do?
16. Describe how the old horse came to ring the bell.
17. Who heard the bell?
18. What did the keeper say to the Governor?
19. What did the Governor do?
20. How did the old horse spend the rest of his days?

QUESTIONS ON THE INTERESTING FACTS.

1. (*a*) What food should you give to a pony?
   (*b*) How should you offer him a lump of sugar?
   (*c*) How should you clean a pony?

THE BELL OF ATRI

2. (a) When should you train a dog in good habits?
   (b) Never interfere with him when he is .... or ....
   (c) What should he have around his neck?
3. (a) What food should you give to a cat?
   (b) Where should she always be kept at night?
   (c) How does a cat clean herself?
4. (a) What is the name given to a tame rabbit's home?
   (b) What food should you give to a rabbit?
   (c) How should you lift a rabbit?
5. (a) Where should you keep a tortoise?
   (b) Where does he like to be in winter?
   (c) What food should you give to a tortoise?
6. (a) Why is the parrot the most amusing pet of all?
   (b) Where can you get his food?
   (c) What should you do at night-time?
7. (a) What food should you give to a canary?
   (b) What should be changed every day?
   (c) On what does he like to sharpen and clean his beak?
8. (a) What is a budgerigar sometimes called?
   (b) What can this little bird be taught to do?
   (c) He is very fond of playing with little ....
9. (a) Where should a goldfish be kept?
   (b) What food should you give to a goldfish?
   (c) See that there is no danger from ....
10. (a) Where are minnows found?
    (b) How do you catch them?
    (c) What food should you give to minnows?

DEVELOPMENT EXERCISES

1. If treated kindly, many creatures become friendly.
   Name two animals, two birds, and two fishes, which make good pets.
2. The bell pealed.
   Put the name of a suitable object in each empty space.
   (1) The .... creaked.   (2) The .... ticked.

13 READER—C

 (3) The .... tinkled. (4) The .... rattled.
 (5) The .... chimed.
3. The horse carried heavy loads.
 Name three other animals which man has trained to pull or carry heavy loads for him.
4. Find the missing word in each of the following. No. 1 is done for you.
 (1) small, smaller, **smallest**. (2) beginning, middle, ...
 (3) breakfast, ..., supper. (4) ...., afternoon, evening.
 (5) Sun, moon, ... (6) metres, centimetres,............
5. The horse **limped** slowly along the road.
 In each of the sentences below, replace the word **walked** by a better word from this list :—prowled, marched, toddled, stamped, hobbled.
 (1) The little child **walked** towards his mother.
 (2) The soldiers **walked** smartly down the street.
 (3) The burglar **walked** through the house.
 (4) The injured man **walked** painfully across the room.
 (5) He **walked** out in a terrible rage.
6. Write short sentences, one for each word, to show correct use of :—
 almost, already, all right, although, always.
7. The governor was **kind** but the merchant was **cruel**.
 Re-write the following sentences giving the **opposites** of the words underlined :—
 (1) The road was long and narrow.
 (2) The horse became thin and weak
 (3) The weather was warm and dry.
 (4) The boy came first and early.
 (5) The well was shallow and empty.
8. The old horse lives in a **meadow**.
 What is a (1) meadow, (2) forest, (3) beach, (4) marsh, (5) moor ?

SAINT ANDREW OF SCOTLAND

SAINT ANDREW is the patron saint of Scotland and the thirtieth of November is Saint Andrew's Day. He is that Andrew who was one of the twelve apostles and a brother of Simon Peter. Although his name does not appear often in the Bible we know that he was a very kind and good man.

Many stories are told of his great kindness and in some of these tales he is described as a brave and fearless knight. The following story about him sounds like a fairy tale but it gives us the picture of a good man who tried to bring happiness to others.

On one of his journeys Saint Andrew reached Thracia (now a part of Greece), a land of much beauty with green meadows and great forests. After a day of long travel he came at last to the foot of a high hill, on top of which stood a great castle.

Although footsore and weary, Saint Andrew climbed the rocky path until he reached the castle gate. There, to his surprise, he saw the body of a huge giant lying upon a rock. He approached very carefully, only to find that the giant was dead.

Puzzled by this discovery Saint Andrew entered the open gate. He kept his sword ready in his hand for he expected every moment to meet some fierce knight of the castle. But no such thing happened ... not a soul was to be seen.

Suddenly he heard voices and ran in the direction of the sounds. There, in a large courtyard, Saint Andrew came across the Thracians offering their prayers to the gods they worshipped ... the sun, the moon, and the stars.

The king sat with his knights around him, yet there was no joy but only sorrow in their hearts. The disciple knew that there was something far wrong so he asked the king what had caused such sadness.

The king told how the evil giant had done many cruel deeds to his people, and how at last the wicked monster tried to kill his six beautiful daughters. In order to protect his daughters, he had called on the gods for help, and they had saved the princesses by changing them into swans.

The king took Saint Andrew to the wall of the castle and pointed to six milk-white swans swimming gracefully in the river far below.

"There are my six daughters," said the king. "The cruel giant is now dead but the princesses still lie under the spell which the gods cast over them. In spite of all our prayers, my poor girls cannot come back to us. It is now seven long years since I left the palace to come and stay here by the banks of this river."

"Most noble king," replied Saint Andrew. "No wonder you are so unhappy. You and your people worship false gods who cannot help you in distress. Tomorrow I will fight against your bravest knights to prove it."

The disciple spent the night in prayer and when dawn came he made ready for the struggle. He wore his colours on his breast—a silver cross set in blue silk.

The contests were fierce and long but Saint Andrew defeated all those who fought against him. The king promised not to worship false gods any more, and no sooner was the promise made than his six daughters came running from the river towards him.

The king's heart was now full of joy and he and his knights were delighted to leave this place of sorrow. When morning came, they marched gaily back to the palace and received a great welcome from the people.

Another interesting story about Saint Andrew tells how he became the patron saint of Scotland.

It so happened that, when Saint Andrew was put to death, his remains were buried in Greece. Some time later a monk named Regulus had a very strange dream. He dreamed that an angel came to him and said, "Regulus! Take the bones of Saint Andrew and carry them to a far country."

"To which country?" asked Regulus.

"I cannot tell you," replied the angel, "but make ready and sail away from this place."

Regulus did as he was told and, with two other monks, sailed on day after day until they reached the coast of Scotland. A great storm arose and the ship was wrecked. Luckily, Regulus and his two friends were saved and they built a church near the place where they landed. The place is now called Saint Andrews.

Regulus stayed in Scotland and preached to the Scots. One night, when they were preparing to fight against their enemies, it is said that a great white cross was seen in the sky. Next day they won the battle and many of them thought that Saint Andrew had helped them to victory.

To show their thanks, the Scots walked to Saint Andrews and worshipped in the little church there. Ever since that day Saint Andrew has been the patron saint of Scotland.

QUESTIONS ON THE STORY.

1. When is Saint Andrew's Day?
2. Why is Saint Andrew mentioned in the Bible?
3. How is the saint described in some of the stories?
4. On one of his journeys he reached the land of ―――――
5. What stood on top of one of the high hills?
6. What did he find at the castle gate?
7. What did he see and hear in the courtyard?
8. Who had tried to kill the king's daughters?
9. From whom had the king asked help?
10. How had the gods saved the princesses?
11. Although the giant was dead, why was the king still sad?
12. What did Saint Andrew say to the king?

14 READER—C

13. What was the result of the fights between Saint Andrew and the knights?
14. What happened when the king promised not to worship false gods?
15. Where were the remains of Saint Andrew first buried?
16. What strange dream had Regulus?
17. What did he do?
18. Where was the ship wrecked?
19. What did the Scots see in the sky on the night before a battle?
20. How did they show their thanks for victory?

THE SEA

SPLASHING, dashing, restless sea,
   Never still you seem to be :
Sometimes angry, sometimes sad,
Sometimes you laugh as though you're glad.
Little children love you well,
Love all the wondrous tales you tell ;
Love to watch you come and go,
In the tides that ebb and flow.

Though so strong and great you are,
Stretching deep, and wide, and far,
Tiny vessels safe you keep,
Rocking them gently, as to sleep,
Wild and rough though you may be,
When you are angry, mighty sea,
When the storm has gone, we find
You are still our playmate kind.

Cecily E. Pike

A STRANGE WARNING

A GREAT many years ago there was a war between the Austrians and the Turks ... one of the many fierce wars that were fought between the Christians and the followers of Mohammed. The Turks attacked and advanced until they reached and surrounded the capital city of Vienna. At the time of the story, the gates of the city had been closed for weeks, and the sentries on the tops of the high walls were carefully watching every movement of the enemy.

The people were in despair as they could get no food from the country, and what little they had within the city could last only a few days more. If they did not surrender, they would die of hunger; and if they did surrender, they would certainly be put to death by the Turks. It seemed as if nothing could save them from the dreadful fate that must come upon them.

Then a very strange thing happened. By good fortune, it turned out to be a warning which saved the city.

One evening, a hard-working baker was in his bakehouse preparing some flour that had to be made into bread for the next day. Suddenly he heard a slight rattling sound behind him. He turned quickly but the noise stopped. Curious to know what it was, the baker stood still and listened carefully. Again he heard the rattle. He walked quietly over to a table on the other side of the bake-house and discovered the cause of the noise.

There on the floor, in a corner below the table, stood a toy drum which belonged to one of his little boys. On the head of the drum lay several marbles. The baker watched it very closely. Every few seconds, the head of the drum would shake, and the little marbles would dance and rattle upon it as if they were alive.

He bent down and put his ear to the ground. Yes, he could now hear the cause of the shaking. It was a regular tapping noise and he wondered what it meant. Suddenly a thought flashed through his mind . . . the strange tapping sounds were caused by the blows of a pick in the earth below. The Turks were digging a tunnel under the walls into the city.

In great haste, the baker went to tell the rulers of the city what he had discovered. They at once told the general in command of the soldiers, and he looked into the matter carefully for himself. He came to the bakehouse, bent his ear to the ground, heard the tapping noise, and watched the marbles dancing on the drum. He agreed that the sound was caused by the enemy digging a tunnel under them.

By means of this warning, the general was able to defeat the Turks. Late that night his soldiers suddenly opened the city gates, and made a surprise attack on the enemy. After a short but fierce fight the Turks turned and fled, and thus the city was saved.

When the war was over, the baker was ordered to appear before the emperor. "I understand," said the king, "that we all owe our safety to you. The little drum and marbles gave you the warning of danger, and you found out the reason. Now, my good man! What do you wish as a reward?"

"Your Majesty!" replied the baker, "I am a humble man and I do not desire riches or rank. Grant

A STRANGE WARNING

me one wish and I will be happy. Let me, from now on, make my bread in the shape of the crescent on the Turkish flag, so that those who eat it will remember our great victory."

The emperor was greatly surprised at this strange wish, but he granted it at once with a smile. "A splendid idea!" said the king. "Remember to send the first bread you make to the palace, so that I will be the first to enjoy it."

Needless to say, the baker was kept busy and happy. His new crescent-shaped bread was called a "Vienna Roll," and so great was the demand for it that he soon made a fortune.

(Adapted)

READER—C

INTERESTING PICTURES ABOUT WARNING SIGNALS

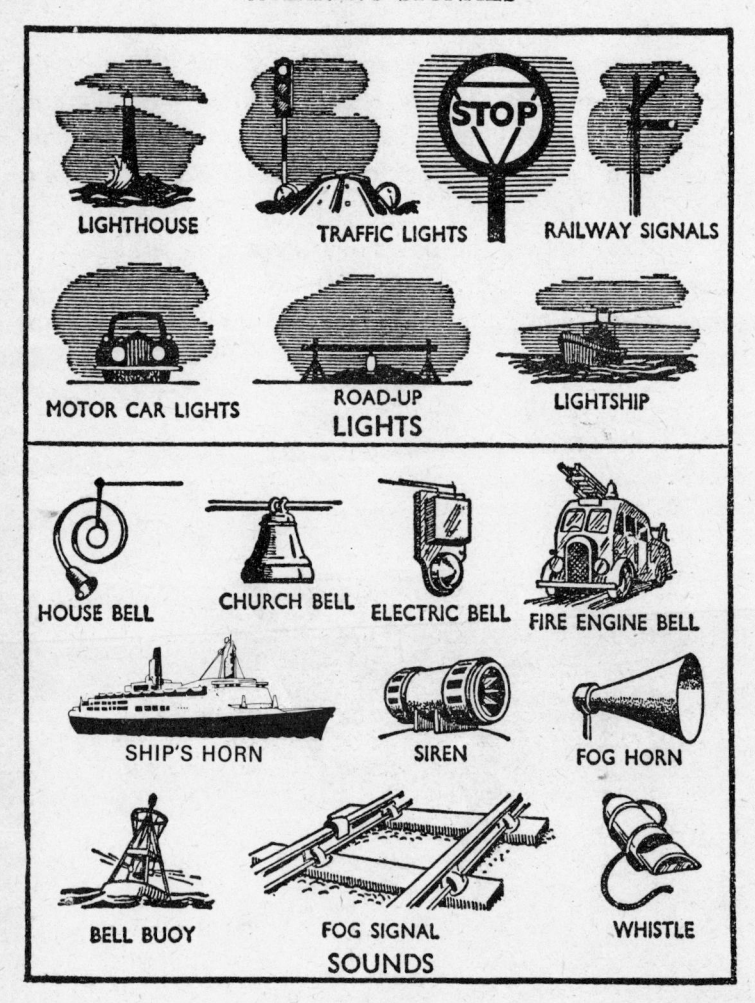

LIGHTHOUSE   TRAFFIC LIGHTS   RAILWAY SIGNALS

MOTOR CAR LIGHTS   ROAD-UP   LIGHTSHIP

LIGHTS

HOUSE BELL   CHURCH BELL   ELECTRIC BELL   FIRE ENGINE BELL

SHIP'S HORN   SIREN   FOG HORN

BELL BUOY   FOG SIGNAL   WHISTLE

SOUNDS

A STRANGE WARNING

QUESTIONS ON THE STORY.

1. What is the title of the story ?
2. Who were fighting ?
3. In what city did the story take place ?
4. Why were the people in despair ?
5. What would happen if they did not surrender ?
6. What would happen if they did surrender ?
7. What was the baker doing ?
8. What made him stop his work ?
9. What was the cause of the noise ?
10. What did he hear when he put his ear to the ground ?
11. What thought flashed through his mind ?
12. To whom did he run to tell of his discovery ?
13. Who came to look carefully into the matter ?
14. What did his soldiers do that same night ?
15. What was the result ?
16. Who ordered the baker to appear before him ?
17. What did the king say to him ?
18. What strange wish did the baker make ?
19. What was the emperor's answer ?
20. What name was given to the crescent-shaped bread ?

QUESTIONS ON THE INTERESTING PICTURES.

1. What three colours do crossing lights show ?
2. A lighthouse protects .... from danger.
3. Who watches railway signals very carefully ?
4. How do lights help a motor-driver at night ?
5. Why must a ship show lights at night ?
6. Why does a motor-driver sound his horn ?
7. What do you do when the house-bell rings ?
8. Why is a fire-alarm very helpful ?
9. Why does a railway-engine always whistle just before it leaves a station ?
10. When is a ship's siren used for protection ?

DEVELOPMENT EXERCISES

1. The baker's son had a toy drum.
   Name three toys which girls like and three toys which boys like.

2. The king is the head of a country.
   Who is the head of a (1) football team, (2) school, (3) ship, (4) church, (5) railway station?

3. A baker works in a bakehouse or bakery.
   Where do these people work? ... farmer, miller, miner, grocer, sailor, shepherd, nurse, porter, conductress, clerk.

4. The Austrians belong to Austria and the Turks belong to Turkey.
   To which countries do the following peoples belong? .. Irish, English, Scottish, Welsh, French, German, Spanish, Indian, Chinese, Dutch.

5. A baker uses an oven at his work.
   Who uses at his work :—(1) hammer and anvil, (2) tractor and plough, (3) comb and scissors, (4) needle and thread, (5) chisel and saw, (6) leather and last, (7) pick and shovel, (8) flag and whistle?

6. You have all seen or heard of crossing lights.
   (a) What does the red light mean?
   (b) What does the amber light mean?
   (c) What does the green light mean?

7. The baker made a special kind of bread called "Vienna Rolls."
   Here are three titles .... Loaf .... Cake .... Biscuit.
   Under each title write down as many different kinds as you can.

8. The Austrians won a victory but the Turks suffered a defeat.
   Give words opposite in meaning to the following words in the story :—short, opened, high, day, quickly, happy, found, under, remember, many, fierce, alive, noise, head, safety, floor, busy, humble, attacked, advanced.

THE BROWNIE

"TU-whit-tu-whoo!" A dear old brown owl sat on a branch in the soft moonlight crooning her strange cry. She had great big deep eyes that could see even through the dark, and though many people were afraid of her, she was really quite harmless and full of fun. She could see a joke and her "Tu-whit-tu-whoo" often ended in a gurgle of laughter.

In a little house nearby there lived a man and his wife and their two children, Tommy and Betty. Though the mother loved both her children, she often had to find fault with them, because they were lazy, forgetful, and untidy. They used to rush about the place, yelling and playing their games, upsetting the furniture, breaking the crockery, spoiling their clothes, and causing a great deal of trouble. They never thought what a bother they were to other people so long as they had a good time.

Then one day mother told them how different it had been in years gone by, when the Brownies used to visit the house.

"What is a Brownie?" they asked.

"A Brownie," answered the mother, "was a little fairy, either a boy or a girl, who came to the house early every morning before anyone was awake. He swept the floor, lit the fire, drew the water, and made ready the breakfast. He also tidied the rooms, weeded the garden, cleaned the boots and shoes, and put the children's clothes into neat bundles. The Brownie did every kind of work, but nobody ever saw him as he slipped away before the people of the house awoke. Everybody was happy and the home was always bright and clean."

Tommy and Betty wanted to know how they could get a Brownie to come and help in their house so as to save them from doing many odd jobs. Mother told them to seek and ask the wise old owl, as she knew everything about fairies, and could tell them where to look for a Brownie.

After dark, the two children went into the wood to find the brown owl. Tommy led the way very bravely at first, but as the path in the silent woods, became darker and darker, he began to feel sorry that he had

THE BROWNIE

started on the adventure. Presently they heard the hooting of the owl among the trees. It sounded so queer that for a moment they wanted to turn and run back home. Gathering all her courage, Betty went forward to the tree in which the owl was sitting.

"Mrs. Owl! Mrs. Owl! We have come to see you!" she cried.

"I am delighted to hear it," replied the wise old bird. "What can I do for you?"

Betty and Tommy told her their troubles; how they were always bothered by having work to do when they wished to play, and how they had heard of the Brownies and wanted to get one to do all the odd jobs for them.

"Tu-whit-tu-whoo!" chuckled the owl. "Do you see that pool down there, Betty? Go to it when the moon is bright, turn round three times, and then say:

Twist me and turn me and show me the elf.
I looked in the water and there saw . . . .'

To get the missing word look down into the water and there you will see the Brownie."

Next evening when the moon was up, Betty went to the pool, turned herself round three times and cried :

"*Twist me and turn me and show me the elf.*
I looked in the water and there saw . . . "

When she looked in the pool she saw nothing except her own reflection. She went back to the owl and told her that she had seen no one there. She had hoped to find the Brownie who would come to the house and do all the work.

" Did you see anyone whose name would fit the words that I gave you ? " said the owl.

" No one," answered Betty.

" Whom did you see in the water ? " asked Mrs. Owl.

" No one but myself," replied Betty.

" Tu-whit-tu-whoo ! " cried the owl. " Would not the word ' *myself* ' fit ? "

Betty repeated the lines again

"*Twist me and turn me and show me the elf.*
I looked in the water and there saw **Myself.**"

" But I am not a Brownie ! " she exclaimed.

Mrs. Owl replied, " No, but you *can* be one if you try. You are a strong and smart little girl. You could sweep the floor ; you are clever enough to lay a fire and light it ; you could fill the kettle and put it on to boil ; you could tidy up the room and set out the breakfast things ; you could make your bed and clean your shoes and fold up your clothes. You could do all these things before any one else was up, so that when

THE BROWNIE

your father and mother came down, they would be surprised and delighted."

Next morning Betty and Tommy slipped out of their beds before anyone was up. They cleaned the house, lit the fire, prepared the breakfast, and crept quietly back to their rooms. When their father and mother came down, expecting to have to do all the work as usual, they were astonished to find that everything was already done for them.

Day after day this went on, and the children had far more fun and enjoyment out of doing their duty like Brownies than they had ever got out of playing rowdy games or being idle. Their home was always bright and clean, and everybody was happy.

(Adapted)

INTERESTING FACTS ON HOME HELP

1. Washing
Before washing your face, bare your arms and neck. Rub your face, neck, ears, hands, wrists, and arms with warm soapy water. Wash again with cold water and dry with a clean towel.

2. Head
Rub your head and hair with warm soapy water until it is thoroughly cleaned. Rinse with warm water and then with cold water to get rid of the soap. Rub well with a warm dry towel. Keep your hair tidy by combing and brushing it as often as possible.

3. Teeth
Rub your teeth with a wet tooth-brush. Put some tooth-paste on the brush and again rub the teeth. Make sure that you get into all the corners between the teeth. Rinse brush and give a final clean. Rinse your mouth with cool fresh water.

4. Clothes
You should brush your clothes every morning and evening. At night-time fold your clothes and place them

THE BROWNIE

in a neat pile, ready for the morning. Take off wet clothing as soon as you can, because you may catch a chill.

5. Shoes
(*a*) Take off all dust or dried mud with a hard brush.
(*b*) Put on a thin layer of boot-polish with a small soft brush.
(*c*) When dry, polish with a large soft brush.
(*d*) To get a very bright shine, rub with a velvet or soft silk pad.

6. Floor
Brush the floor gently but firmly. Sweep all the dust and dirt to one spot where it can be collected easily with a shovel. Make sure that you go into all the corners and remember to brush below the table and chairs.

7. Dishes
Put all scraps of food and tea-leaves into bin.
Fill basin with hot water and add a little soap powder.
Put in dirty dishes and allow them to soak for a minute or two.
Rub dishes in the water with a soft cloth or dish mop.
Take out dishes after cleaning and leave to dry.
Wipe dishes with a soft dry clean cloth.

8. Tea
Fill the kettle with fresh water and put it on to boil. Warm the clean empty tea-pot by rinsing it with hot water. Take the tea-pot to the kettle not the kettle to the tea-pot as it is much safer. When the water is bubbling in the kettle, put tea, one teaspoonful for each person and one more, into the pot. Pour the boiling

water into the tea-pot, and leave to brew for two minutes. The tea is then ready to be poured into the cups.

9. Fire

Pick out the black cinders and place them to one side.
Clear away carefully all dust and useless ashes from the fireplace.
Put on some crumpled paper.
Place some sticks or firelighters criss-cross on the paper.
Put the cinders on top of the sticks or firelighters.
Add some small lumps of coal.
To start the fire, set the paper alight.

10. Errands

When you are asked to go errands to the shops, see that you go and return as quickly as possible. Don't delay or play games on the way. Remember what you were asked to get ; how much the goods cost ; how much money you were given ; and make sure that you have the right change. If you have to get a number of things, make a list of them on a piece of paper.

QUESTIONS ON THE STORY.

1. What is the title of the story ?
2. Describe Mrs. Owl.
3. Give her strange cry.
4. Who lived in the little house near the wood ?
5. What were the names of the two children ?
6. Why was their mother often angry with them ?
7. What is a Brownie ?
8. When did a Brownie visit a house ?
9. What work did he do ?
10. When did the Brownie slip away ?

THE BROWNIE

11. Why did the children want to speak to Mrs. Owl?
12. When did they visit her?
13. What did the wise old bird tell them to do?
14. When did Betty visit the pool?
15. Repeat the two lines of verse.
16. What did Betty see in the pool?
17. What did she expect to see in the pool?
18. What was the missing word?
19. How could the children be like Brownies?
20. What change did it make in their home?

QUESTIONS ON THE INTERESTING FACTS.

1. (a) When washing, what is needed with water to remove the dirt?
   (b) How should you dry yourself?
2. (a) To clean your hair, you should wash your head with............
   (b) How can you keep your hair tidy?
3. (a) What do you use to scrub your teeth?
   (b) What do you put on the brush?
4. (a) What should you do with your clothes before going to bed?
   (b) Why must you take off wet clothing as soon as possible?
5. Describe the best way to clean and polish your shoes.
6. When sweeping a floor, why should you brush all dust and dirt to one spot?
7. When washing dishes, why should the water be hot?
8. Describe the best way to make tea.
9. Describe the best way to set a fire.
10. What should you remember when you are asked to go on an errand?

DEVELOPMENT EXERCISES

1. Re-write the following sentences changing all masculines into feminines.
   (a) The **man** saved the little **boy**.
   (b) **Father** and **uncle** were laughing.
   (c) The **prince** bowed to the **king**.
   (d) My **brother** waved to **him**.
   (e) **He** spoke to the **husband**.
2. The owl says " Tu-whit-tu-whoo."
   What do the following creatures say :—(1) cat, (2) dog, (3) cow, (4) sheep, (5) duck, (6) cock, (7) cuckoo, (8) rook ?
3. The owl could see in the dark.
   Name any other creatures which can see quite well in the dark.
4. What should you use to clean (a) face and hands, (b) teeth, (c) clothes, (d) shoes, (e) floor, (f) dishes ?
5. In what ways can you be polite and well-behaved :—(a) at home, (b) in school, (c) in the street, (d) in a tram-car or bus ?
6. Explain the difference between (a) pen and pencil, (b) shoes and boots, (c) clock and watch, (d) pin and needle, (e) shadow and reflection.
7. Tell what you do from the time you waken in the morning till the time you go to school.
8. You have all heard of " The Brownies." What else can young people join ?

GOD IN A HURRICANE

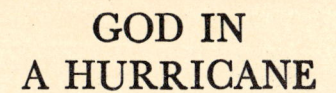

I never knew real Wind,
   Until one August night;
What I called " wind " had only been
   Soft zephyrs without might.

Though I'd heard a tempest blow,
   It proved a gust forsooth;
When THIS WIND SPOKE, I got to know
   The hounds of God let loose!

The attic beams above my head
   Jerked, jarred, jammed!
While giant engines boomed like mad;
   They clutched! They pulled! They rammed!

The rain came driving down in floods!
   It smoked! It poured! It wept!
While tons of Wind pushed at my goods; —
   Outside they tore, and swept!

They pushed! They shoved my poor roof zinc!
   It banged! It knocked! It yelled!
It roared! It shook! I scarce could think!
   I prayed! And that roof HELD!

Nellie Olson

TWO CLEVER BIRDS

IT was early spring and the plover, who was just over a year old, was performing like a wonderful acrobat. Up sailed the bird towards the blue sky and then suddenly he turned and dived down almost to the ground. Up he went again, twisting from side to side The lapwing, as he is sometimes called, was certainly enjoying himself, but he was not doing this for fun.

The plover was courting, and he hoped that a henbird, who was watching him from the ground below, would think him so clever that she would become his mate. Every now and again the flying plover gave a clear whistle. Suddenly he dropped to the earth and landed gracefully beside her. When she did not fly away from him, he knew at once that she also wanted to set up house.

Soon they began to build their nest, which was just a few bits of grass placed inside a hollow beneath a tuft of grass. They were very proud of their little home, and here the hen-bird laid four eggs, dark green in colour.

One day, a boy named John came into the meadow. The plover, who was keeping a sharp look-out while the hen-bird was sitting on the eggs, rose quickly into

TWO CLEVER BIRDS

the air and began to fly about wildly. His mate knew what this meant and, slipping quietly off her eggs, she ran along the ground away from the nest before she too rose into the air.

"Plovers!" cried John. "I wonder if I can find their nest?"

John searched all over the meadow, but he did not find it, because the nest was very cleverly hidden and the eggs were almost the same colour as the grass.

"Pee-wee! Pee-wee!" cried the two plovers over and over again as they flew around. Both birds were very careful not to fly over or near where their nest was.

"It's a shame to worry you like this," said John at last. "Of course, I would not have touched your eggs if I had found them. I only wanted to see your little nest. Good-bye!"

With a wave of his hand to the two plovers the boy went off down the road. When they were quite sure that he had gone away, they flew down to the ground. The birds were again very careful, however, to land some distance away from the nest before they ran to it through the tall grass. When they reached home, the hen-bird at once sat on her eggs.

About an hour or so afterwards, the plover again rose quickly into the air and flew about wildly. This time the danger was much greater than before, because it was their old enemy, the cat. The hen-bird had no chance to slip quietly off her eggs for pussy was too near and would spy the nest.

The plover tried to defend his mate and her eggs by flying this way and that, as close to the cat as he could safely go. Pussy was not afraid, however, and each time the bird came near, she crouched ready to spring.

As the cat approached the nest, the birds tried another trick. The hen-bird suddenly rose from her eggs and fluttered towards a nearby stream. She pretended that she was hurt, and it looked as if one of her wings was broken. Pussy ran after her and expected to catch her quite easily. Suddenly the cat made a wild spring at the bird, but the plover dodged to one side and flew away.

TWO CLEVER BIRDS

Plop! Poor old pussy landed right in the middle of the muddy stream. Cats are not fond of water and they hate wet sticky mud. In a terrible rage she struggled to the bank and then ran home as quickly as she could. The two birds followed her for part of the way and shouted "Pee-wee! Pee-wee!" as if they were laughing at her.

Back again went the plovers to their nest and, I'm glad to say, they were left in peace. Then one fine day the eggs broke, and out of the shells came four little fluffy chicks. For the first week or so, the tiny birds ran after their parents, who fed them on little worms, spiders, and flies. When they were about seven weeks old, the young ones flew away because they were then fully grown and able to look after themselves.

INTERESTING FACTS ABOUT BIRDS' NESTS

Birds sometimes choose very strange places in which to make their nests but they always build their homes near their feeding grounds and in places where they are safe from enemies.

In a Hole in a Tree or in a Bank

The woodpecker and the nuthatch build nests in holes in trees.

The kingfisher and the Jamaican robin red-breast build their nests in holes which they make in banks.

In Moors, Marshes and Swamps

Snipe, reed warblers, curlews, pheasants, grouse, partridges and flamingoes all build their nests mostly out of coarse grass in moors, marshes or swamps.

In Open Fields

Skylarks, wagtails, lapwings, corncrakes and grassquits all nest on open ground or in fields.

In Trees

Rooks, crows, magpies, herons and storks usually build their nests in high trees.

TWO CLEVER BIRDS

In Bushes and Hedges and Banks

Thrushes, sparrows, chaffinches, laughing thrushes and mocking birds build their nests in bushes and hedges.

The robin and wren usually build their homes in mossy banks. The sand-martin digs a tunnel in the face of a sandy bank and makes its nest of straw and feathers at the far end of the hole.

At the Edges of Ponds

The duck, swan and goose build their nests of grass, feathers and leaves among rushes near a pond or lake. The dipper, water-hen and kingfisher make their nests in the banks of streams.

In Buildings

The swallow, jackdaw, starling, swift and house-martin have their nests in buildings.

The barn-owl makes no nest but lays its eggs in corners among the rafters.

On Mountains

The eagle, falcon, raven, hawk and condor make their nests on the ledges of mountains.

On Sea Cliffs

The gannet, kittiwake and cormorant build their homes of grass and sea-weed on the ledges of sea cliffs. The guillemot and razorbill make no nest but lay their eggs in hollows on the ledges. The puffin nests at the end of a burrow dug in the earth at the top of a cliff.

Some birds do not raise their own young. They lay their eggs in other birds' nests, sometimes kicking out one or more of the eggs already there. When hatched the chick makes room for itself by pushing out one of the other nestlings. Such parasite birds in Europe are cuckoos, in America cowbirds, and in Africa honey guides.

QUESTIONS ON THE STORY.

1. What is the title of the story?
2. What season of the year was it?
3. Give another name for the plover.
4. How did he court the hen-bird?
5. Describe their nest.
6. How many eggs did the hen-bird lay?
7. What colour were the eggs?
8. Who came into the meadow one day?
9. What did the plovers do?
10. Why did the boy fail to find the nest?
11. What enemy came an hour or so afterwards?
12. How did the plover try to defend his mate and the eggs?
13. What did the pussy do when the bird came near?
14. How did the hen-bird pretend to be hurt?
15. When pussy sprang, where did she land?
16. Why was the cat very angry?
17. How did the plovers feel?
18. On what did the parent birds feed the little chicks?
19. At what age were they able to look after themselves?
20. What is the call of the plover?

TWO CLEVER BIRDS

QUESTIONS ON THE INTERESTING FACTS.

1. Name any bird which nests on the ground in an open field.
2. Which bird makes a nest of coarse grass in a marsh?
3. Name a bird which builds a nest in a thick hedge or bush.
4. (*a*) Which bird nests in the top of a high tree?
   (*b*) Name a bird which likes to nest in a hole in a tree.
5. (*a*) Which bird usually makes its nest in a mossy bank?
   (*b*) Describe a sand-martin's nest.
6. (*a*) Where does a swan build its nest?
   (*b*) Describe a kingfisher's nest.
7. Name a bird which makes its home in a building.
8. Where does the eagle build its huge nest?
9. (*a*) Name a bird which makes a nest of grass and sea-weed on a cliff.
   (*b*) Describe a puffin's nest.
10. (*a*) Which bird lays her egg in another bird's nest?
    (*b*) What does the young cuckoo do to the other nestlings?

DEVELOPMENT EXERCISES

1. A bird's home is called a **nest**.
   Name the homes of :—dog, horse, pig, cow, tame rabbit, bee, hen, owl, eagle, tame pigeon.
2. Which bird (1) has a red breast? (2) is able to talk? (3) hunts at night? (4) is a lovely singer? (5) has a white waistcoat?
3. Name two birds which are often seen (*a*) in city streets, (*b*) swimming in streams or ponds, (*c*) in the woods, (*d*) at the seaside.
4. A young bird is called a **nestling**.
   What name is given to a young (1) hen, (2) duck, (3) goose, (4) eagle, (5) owl?

5. Name a bird which has (1) webbed feet, (2) big staring eyes, (3) long legs, (4) a hooked beak, (5) big tail feathers.
6. Write down these titles .... Animals .... Birds .... Flowers. Read the list below and write each word under the title to which it belongs.

    cuckoo, violet, camel, rabbit, tulip, wren, reindeer, crocus, ostrich, snowdrop, swan, kangaroo, zebra, stork, buttercup.
7. We say "As wise as an owl."

    Fill in the blank spaces below from the following list of birds:—

    swan, hawk, lark, raven, peacock, chicken.

    (a) as happy as a .... (b) as swift as a ....
    (c) as tender as a .... (d) as graceful as a ....
    (e) as black as a .... (f) as proud as a ....

8. Describe the different ways in which these birds fly:—lark, seagull, crow, swallow, hawk.

SAINT PATRICK OF IRELAND

SAINT PATRICK is the patron saint of Ireland and the seventeenth of March is Saint Patrick's Day. Everywhere in that country, and among Irish people in all parts of the world, his name is still cherished and yet—strange to say—he was not an Irishman.

He was born near Dumbarton in Scotland and later the family removed to a farm on the Scottish side of the Solway Firth. Across the sea could be seen the distant coast of Ireland.

One night, when Patrick was about sixteen years of age, several strange boats sailed up the Solway. Suddenly, and without any warning, they made for the shore.

Out of the ships leapt fierce bearded warriors who had come to steal, to burn, and to kill. Some of the people managed to escape from these terrible pirates, but many were captured. Patrick was one of those who were caught and taken on board the ships. That was how he first went to Ireland—a poor miserable slave.

On their return from this raid, the Irish sea-robbers sold Patrick to Milchu, the chief of a small warlike clan. Milchu made him a swineherd and so the young lad had to look after the pigs. Sometimes he was sent out to the hills to watch the sheep, and often he would lie out under the stars and think of his home and those he loved. For six long years Patrick endured this hard rough life, always serving his master faithfully and well.

One evening, while sleeping on the hillside, he had a strange dream in which a voice said to him, " Your prayers are answered. The ship has come." When he awoke, he felt certain that he was no longer to be a slave, and set off at once towards the coast. For two hundred weary miles, Patrick struggled on bravely until he reached the sea, near where Sligo now stands. There, to his great joy, he found a ship which was almost ready to sail for France.

Patrick went up to the captain of the ship and said, "I would like to go with you to France."

"Have you any money or goods to pay your fare?" asked the captain.

"No. I have nothing. I will work hard on board your ship and so repay you," replied Patrick.

"In that case you can't sail with us. Be off with you!" said the captain roughly.

Patrick walked away a little distance, and then turned to watch the sailors, who were trying to get some big Irish wolfhounds on board. The frightened dogs were snapping and snarling as the men dragged them along.

As one of the dogs passed, Patrick laid his hand on the animal's head and spoke quietly. The dog stopped barking at once and tried to lick his hand. The captain noticed what had happened and as Patrick was about to leave he heard footsteps behind him. It was one of the sailors.

"Come back," said the man. "The captain wants to speak to you."

When Patrick returned, the captain said to him, "I have changed my mind. You can come with us if you look after the dogs on the voyage."

Patrick thanked him and ran joyfully aboard. The ship took three days to reach France and, when he arrived, Patrick went to stay with his uncle who was a famous bishop. It was then that he made up his mind to become a priest.

One night, while the young man was asleep, an angel came to him and held out a letter. Patrick read the words on it: "The Voice of the Irish" and then he heard children's voices calling "Come and walk among us again." When Patrick awoke he knew that he must return some day to Ireland and so he spent the next few years training hard as a priest.

Once more, in 432 A.D., Patrick set sail for Ireland—not as a slave this time—but as a bishop. When he and his friends landed, they did not receive a very friendly welcome, and it was some time before the people would listen to them.

Patrick had many adventures as he travelled from place to place preaching the gospel. One story tells how,

SAINT PATRICK OF IRELAND

by beating a drum on his journeys through the land, he drove all the snakes and serpents into the sea and now none of these creatures are to be seen there.

(*Adapted*)

QUESTIONS ON THE STORY.

1. What is the title of the story?
2. Where was Saint Patrick born?
3. To which part of the country did the family go later?
4. From their home, what could they see across the sea?
5. Who came sailing quietly up the Solway?
6. What had they come to do?
7. What was Saint Patrick when he first went to Ireland?
8. To whom did the sea-robbers sell the young lad?
9. What was Saint Patrick's first job?
10. What strange message did he receive one night?
11. How far did he walk to reach the coast?
12. There, to his great joy, he saw..
13. Tell the story of Saint Patrick and the dogs.
14. How long did the voyage take?
15. Where did the young man go to stay when he arrived?
16. What did he make up his mind to become?
17. Tell the story of his strange dream.
18. What was Saint Patrick when he went to Ireland the second time?
19. In what year did Saint Patrick return to Ireland?
20. Which creatures were said to have been driven into the sea by him?

THE LIGHTHOUSE

BURNING upon some hidden shore,
    Across the sea one night,
"A little reef," the Captain said,
    We saw a shining light.

He said there was a lighthouse there,
    Where, lonely in the sea,
Men lived to guard that moving light,
    And trim the lamp for me.

For me, for him, for every ship,
    That passes by that way.
I thought it must be strange and quiet,
    To be there every day.

They have no shops, no fields, no streets,
    No whispering sound of trees,
But always shouting at their feet,
    The great voice of the seas.

And when we sleep at night they wake,
    And over every wave,
They send that straight long arm of light,
    Stretched like a rope to save.

Marjory Wilson.

THE TWO BROTHERS

ONCE upon a time there lived two brothers who, when they were children, were always together. They grew to be handsome young men, and at last the time came when they had to part and make their own ways in life.

One day the elder brother said to the younger, "Choose what you wish to do in life, and may God bless your choice. I am going to the King's palace. Nothing will please me but to serve him and my country."

"Good fortune and a blessing go with you," replied the younger brother. "I too should like to serve my King and country, but I am not so clever a scholar as you. To hammer a shoe from the glowing iron while the red fire roars and the anvil rings ... that is the work I like best. I want to be a blacksmith, even as my father was before me."

The two brothers shook hands and went on their different ways; nor did they meet again till many a year had come and gone.

The elder brother, as he said he would, went to serve at the palace, and in time he won great fame and became a trusted friend of the King.

The younger brother built a lovely little cottage with a blacksmith's shop by the side of a road, and there he worked merrily from early morn till the stars shone at night. He was known by three different names: the Mighty Blacksmith because of his great strength; the Honest Blacksmith because he charged no more than his work was worth; and the Master Blacksmith because no other smith in the land could shoe a horse so well or so speedily. He was always bright and cheerful and, as he worked, his hammer seemed to sing to him :

> *Cling, clang, cling !*
> *Cling, clang, cling !*
> *He who works his very best*
> *Is fit to serve the King.*

One sad day, news came to the King that the ruler of another kingdom was getting ready to fight against him and his people. There was great excitement in the land and the King was very worried.

THE TWO BROTHERS

Some people at the palace wanted him to gather a large army and march at once against the enemy. "If we do not make war upon him, he will make war upon us," they said.

The King's true friends loved peace, and among these was the elder brother.

"Let me ride alone to the other King's palace," said the brother, "and there I will learn from the King himself whether he is our friend or foe. I do not believe most of the stories that are going about, and it is much easier to begin a fight than to end one."

The King was well pleased with the elder brother and said, "Go as soon as you are ready, but remember that if you do not return by the peal of the bells at noon on the day before Christmas, then those that want war shall have their way."

Off went the brother on his long journey. When he arrived, he found that the stories had been false and the ruler gave him a message of goodwill to take back to his King.

The trouble started on his way back. A great storm raged over the land and he lost his way several times.

Day and night he rode, and only when his horse tired, did he stop to rest. At dawn on the day before Christmas he was still thirty miles from the palace.

Then came the worst blow. The brave horse, that had done so well, lost a shoe. The rider bowed his head upon the saddle and wept, for he did not know where to go for help.

Suddenly he heard a distant sound that was sweeter than music to his ears :

"*Cling, clang, cling !*
Cling, clang, cling !"

He shouted joyfully and cried, " Only a blacksmith plays that tune ! " On he hurried and it was not long before he reached the smithy.

" Smith, smith ! If you love your country, shoe my horse as quickly as you can ! " cried the horseman.

" Certainly, sir ! " replied the smith. " I'll take only a few minutes."

The smith rushed to his fire and set to work. Soon the horse was shod and ready for the road again.

" Thank you, smith ! You have served your King well this day. What do I owe you ? "

" You owe me nothing," said the smith. " To serve my King and country is pay enough for me."

The two men stared at one another, and each saw that the other was his brother.

THE TWO BROTHERS

"God bless you, brother!" and "God speed you, brother!" was all that they had time to say, for the elder brother mounted his horse and was off like the wind.

At the palace the King waited hopefully for the message, but as the day came almost to noon, he turned slowly to his men and sadly shook his head.

"Shall we not saddle our horses and call out the soldiers?" said those who wanted war.

"No!" cried the others. "You must wait till the bells have rung."

Suddenly a sentry rushed into the room. "Your Majesty! I see a horseman coming towards the palace at great speed. It must be the news we expect."

Just as the bells began to ring, the elder brother entered, bowed to the King, and handed him the message. The King tore it open and read:

"*A Merry Christmas to you my friend,*
 And peace and goodwill to all your people."

Never was there such rejoicing in the land. The King gave rich rewards to the elder brother, who would not take any of them for himself alone.

"I would have failed, had it not been for my brother, the blacksmith, who shod my horse to-day. If it please your Majesty, half of all that you give to me I will give to him."

"Your wish is granted," said the King. "Two good servants are better than one. Bring your brother to me that I may thank him also."

The two brothers lived very happily . . . each doing the work he liked best. The elder brother stayed in his castle and faithfully served the King at the palace. The younger brother was content to stay in his little cottage, but he built a bigger and better smithy.

THE TWO BROTHERS

INTERESTING PICTURES
OF
DIFFERENT HOMES.

QUESTIONS ON THE STORY.

1. What is the title of the story ?
2. What did the elder brother want to be ?
3. What did the younger brother want to be ?
4. What kind of home did the younger brother build ?
5. By what three names was the blacksmith known ?
6. Why was he called these names ?
7. What did the hammer seem to sing to him ?
8. Why was there great excitement in the land ?
9. What did the foolish people want to do ?
10. What did the elder brother say to the King ?
11. By what time was he to return to the palace ?
12. Why was he so long on his way back ?
13. What happened to his horse ?
14. What distant sound did he hear ?
15. How long did the blacksmith take to shoe the horse ?
16. What payment did the blacksmith take for his work ?
17. What did they both suddenly discover ?
18. What reply did one King send to the other ?
19. What did the elder brother do with his reward ?
20. Where did the brothers live happily ?

QUESTIONS ON THE PICTURES

1. Who lives in a palace ?
2. Why did a castle have strong high walls ?
3. What is usually round a mansion ?
4. How do you enter a tenement ?
5. Describe a villa.
6. What kind of house is a bungalow ?
7. Where is a cottage usually to be seen ?
8. What kind of house is a " pre-fab " ?
9. What is a caravan ?
10. Where do you see a houseboat ?

THE TWO BROTHERS

DEVELOPMENT EXERCISES

1. A blacksmith shoes horses.
   Who (a) makes bread, (b) delivers letters, (c) grows crops, (d) mends pipes, (e) serves meals?
2. Twelve o'clock mid-day is called *noon*.
   (a) Twelve o'clock at night is called ....
   (b) Seven days is called a ....
   (c) Twelve months is called a ....
   (d A hundred years is called a ....
   (e) Two weeks is called a ....
3. The blacksmith lived in a cottage.
   Whom would you expect to find living in a (1) palace, (2) barracks, (3) snow-house, (4) wigwam, (5) prison?
4. The elder brother rode off like the wind.
   Complete the following :—
   (a) The boy could climb like a ....
   (b) The girl could swim like a ....
   (c) The boy could run like a ....
   (d) The girl could sing like a ....
   (e) The glutton could eat like a ....
5. The blacksmith used a hammer and anvil.
   (a) The boy used a .... to sharpen the pencil.
   (b) The man used a .... to dig the garden.
   (c) The girl used a .... to sweep the floor.
   (d) The joiner used a .... to smooth the wood.
   (e) The engineer used a .... to tighten the nuts.
6. Complete the following. No. 1 is done for you.
   (1) younger-*elder*, (2) smaller-...................., (3) slower-....................,
   (4) shorter-...................., (5) thinner-...................., (6) earlier-....................
7. The two men in the story were *brothers*.
   What name do you give to your father or mother's (a) sister, (b) brother, (c) mother, (d) father?

8. The *peal* of bells.
   Put the following words in their proper places:—
   clatter, screeching, tramp, jingle, beating.
   (a) the.................of feet.
   (b) the.................of drums.
   (c) the.................of hoofs.
   (d) the.................of brakes.
   (e) the.................of spurs.

SILK

IS it not strange that tiny little worms can give us the soft smooth shining silk from which our most beautiful clothing is made? No one knows who discovered that the silkworm could be used to clothe people. For thousands of years, however, men have kept millions and millions of these small creatures working away, spinning the silk threads that are used to make many kinds of beautiful things.

At first the making of silk was kept a great secret. The kings of China warned their people not to teach strangers the way in which it was done They even gave orders that no silkworm eggs were to be allowed out of the country, and that any one breaking the rules would be severely punished.

In spite of these laws the silk industry gradually spread. It is said that a princess, who left to marry a prince in another country, hid some of the eggs in her head-dress and carried them to her new home. She taught the people how to make silk and in a few years the secret of silkworms and silk weaving became known in many other lands. Here is the secret which was kept so well for hundreds of years.

The silk moth lays eggs in the early summer and dies soon after laying them. In its wild state the moth lays its eggs on the leaves of the mulberry tree; but men discovered that it would also lay them on sheets of paper or muslin. These sheets are hung up in a cool place until the following spring. At that time of the year the mulberry leaves are young and tender and so make perfect food.

What a curious sight these sheets of eggs are! Each egg is only the size of a pin head. Often the eggs are sold at so much an ounce.

When hatching time comes, the eggs are kept in a warm place. Tiny hair-like worms, about a quarter of an inch long, come out of the eggs. They are very hungry and at once begin eating the mulberry leaves. For eight or nine days these little gluttons eat on steadily. Then they stop eating and take a long sleep. When they wake, they crawl from their old skins and come out with new ones. Again they eat like gluttons for several days.

At last, when they have had four of these long sleeps, they are ready to spin their shells or cocoons. By this time they have grown from hair-like worms to caterpillars three inches long and about as thick as your finger.

The caterpillar begins to spin a cocoon. The insect sways its head to and fro, and from its mouth comes a sticky gum which hardens into a silk thread when it touches the air. For two or three days the caterpillar continues to wrap this thread round and round its

SILK 23

body. Often the thread is more than a mile long before the little house, in which the caterpillar will change into a moth, is finished.

If the silk-workers left the cocoons alone for two or three weeks, moths would come out of them and the threads would be broken or spoiled. They allow only a small number of worms to become moths. These insects will lay eggs for the following year. All the other cocoons are baked in an oven in order to kill the worms inside.

The silk-workers soak the cocoons in hot water and carefully unwind the threads from them. So fine are the threads that six or seven of them have to be twisted together to make silk strong enough for use. These threads are wound into balls, ready to be woven into cloth either at home or somewhere across the seas.

QUESTIONS ON THE STORY.

1. What is the title of the lesson?
2. What little creature gives us silk?
3. What orders did the kings of China give to their people?
4. What would happen to anyone who broke the laws?
5. Who is said to have taken the secret to another country?
6. How did she do it?
7. When does the silk moth lay her eggs?
8. What size is an egg?
9. Where does she lay them?
10. What happens to the moth soon after laying the eggs?
11. What comes out of the egg in spring?
12. What does the worm eat?
13. What happens after eight or nine days?
14. What do they do when they wake?
15. How many long sleeps do they have?
16. How does the caterpillar make a silk thread?
17. Why are the cocoons baked in an oven?
18. Why are the cocoons later soaked in hot water?
19. Why are six or seven threads twisted together?
20. What articles of clothing worn by the girl and boy on the previous page might be made of silk?

THE PEDLAR'S CARAVAN

I wish I lived in a caravan,
   With a horse to drive, like a pedlar man !
Where he comes from nobody knows,
Or where he goes to, but on he goes !

His caravan has windows two,
And a chimney of tin, that the smoke comes through ;
He has a wife, with a baby brown,
And they go riding from town to town.

Chairs to mend, and delf to sell !
He clashes the basins like a bell ;
Tea-trays, baskets ranged in order,
Plates, with alphabets round the border !

The roads are brown, and the sea is green,
But his house is like a bathing-machine ;
The world is round, and he can ride,
Rumble and splash, to the other side !

With the pedlar man I should like to roam,
And write a book when I came home ;
All the people would read my book,
Just like the Travels of Captain Cook !

W. B. Rands.

GULLS TO THE RESCUE

THIS story is about something that really happened many years ago.

A brave little company of people crossed the plains of North America in big covered waggons with many horses, and finally managed to climb to the top of the Rocky Mountains, and down again on the other side into a great valley.

It was a valley of brown, bare, desert soil, in a place where almost no rain fell ; but the snow on the mountain tops sent down little streams of pure water ; the winds were gentle, and lying at the foot of the hills was a wonderful lake of salt water. The people decided to settle there and so built themselves huts and cabins for the winter.

It had taken them several months to make the terrible journey. Many had died of weariness and illness on the way. The food they had brought in their waggons was nearly finished, and by the time spring had come, they were forced to live on roots dug from the ground.

Their lives now depended on the crops of corn and vegetables which they had sown in the valley. They made the soil fertile by spreading water from the little streams over it,—what we call "irrigating." They

GULLS TO THE RESCUE

planted enough corn and vegetables for all their needs. Everyone helped, and everyone watched for the sprouting shoots, with hopes, and prayers, and careful eyes.

In good time the seeds sprouted, and the dry brown earth was covered with a carpet of green, growing crops. No garden could have looked better than the great fields of that desert valley. From day to day the little shoots grew and flourished till they were all well above the ground.

Then a terrible thing happened. One day, the men who were watering the crops saw a great army of insects swarming over the ground at the edge of the fields nearest the mountains. These insects were crickets, and they were hopping from the stony places into the fields. Worst of all, it was seen that crickets were eating the young green shoots and leaves. More came, and more, and even more, and as they came, they spread out till they covered a large part of the corn field.

The men rushed forward and tried to kill the crickets by stamping on them and beating them with sticks, but the numbers were so great that it was useless. They gave up hope when they saw another huge army of black, hopping, crawling insects streaming down the hillside to destroy the crops.

Tired and weary, the men went to tell the terrible news and all the village came out to help. They made fires; they dug trenches and filled them with water; but it was all in vain. When the people fought the crickets in one place, new armies of insects attacked the fields in other places.

The people cried in despair. A few knelt to pray. They saw that it would mean starvation and death. Others gathered round them and joined them, weeping. Soon everyone was kneeling in the fields, and praying to be rid of the crickets.

Suddenly from far off came the sound of flapping wings. It grew louder and louder. Some of the people looked up in surprise. They saw, like a white cloud rising from the lake, a huge flock of seagulls flying towards them. Snow-white in the sun, with great wings beating, they came in hundreds and hundreds.

"The gulls! the gulls!" was the cry. "What does it mean?"

The gulls flew overhead with a chorus of loud cries, and then, with outspread wings, they swooped down on the corn fields.

"Oh! woe! woe!" cried the people. "The gulls

are joining the crickets and are eating the crops! The crops will be ruined!"

All at once, someone called out,—

"No, no! Look! The gulls are eating the insects! They are *not* eating the crops! They are eating *only* the crickets!"

It was true. The gulls devoured the crickets in dozens, in hundreds, in swarms. They ate until they could eat no more and then flew heavily back to the lake. Soon afterwards they returned with new appetites and gobbled up more and more crickets. When at last they finished, they had cleared the fields of the army of insects, and thus the people were saved.

To this day, in the city of Salt Lake, which grew out of that village, children are taught to love the seagulls. When they learn to draw and paint in the schools, their first picture is often that of a cricket and a gull.

(*Adapted*)

INTERESTING FACTS ABOUT WATER BIRDS.

Water Birds are usually white, black, grey, blue-grey, or a mixture of these four colours. They have webbed feet and have feathers which do not get soaked with water.

1. **Ducks** are of many kinds and colours, and are to be seen on ponds, lakes, and bays. They have flat wide bills and eat insects, frogs, and snails. Although wild ducks are good fliers, tame ducks seldom fly. They make a loud " quacking " noise.

2. **Geese** are very like ducks in appearance, only that they are bigger and have longer necks. They fly in the form of the letter V and have a call which sounds like "kark, kark."

3. **Swans** are larger than ducks or geese and have very long slender necks. They are to be

GULLS TO THE RESCUE

seen sailing slowly through the water, on ponds, rivers, and lakes. When angry they hiss and make a deep trumpeting sound.

4. **Herons** are big grey-and-white birds with long thin necks and legs. They live in marshes but may often be seen standing, still and silent, in the waters of rivers and lakes. There they wait to snap with their sharp-pointed beaks at passing fish. Herons make a deep croaking sound, and eat fish, frogs, eels, and insects.

5. **Gulls** are the most common water birds around lakes and seas. They are often seen gliding gracefully through the air, or floating gently on the surface of the water. Gulls are noisy, hungry birds, and eat insects, fish, worms, and shellfish.

6. **Terns** are sometimes called " Sea swallows," because they have long forked tails and fly like swallows. They eat insects and shellfish and make sounds like " keeri " and " kick."

7. **Pelicans** fly in small flocks. Some dive into the water to catch fishes which they hold in a pouch under their bills. Pelicans are very buoyant due to their hollow bones and the air sacs in their bodies.

8. **Gannets** are very like gulls in appearance, only that they are much bigger. When flying, these birds can see the fish far below in the water, and they dive straight down into the sea with a great splash. The fish, when caught, are swallowed beneath the surface.

9. **Cormorants** are long-necked blackish birds which live on the rocky parts of the coast. They are often to be seen standing on rocks at the foot of cliffs or floating on the sea. These birds dive and swim for a long time under water in search of fish. Cormorants fly close to the surface with their long necks stretched forward.

10. **Penguins** live near the South Pole but can be seen at the zoo. They are expert swimmers but cannot fly. Penguins have been described as birds, black in colour, with a white waistcoat.

QUESTIONS ON THE STORY.
1. What is the title of the story?
2. In which part of the world did the story take place?
3. How did the people travel across the country?
4. How long did it take them to make the journey?

GULLS TO THE RESCUE

5. Where did they decide to settle?
6. What were they forced to do when spring came?
7. What did the people plant in the fields?
8. What word means spreading water over the soil to make it fertile?
9. What terrible thing happened one day?
10. What did this mean to the people?
11. How did the men attack the insects?
12. Why did they give up the struggle?
13. Why did the people kneel on the ground?
14. What sound did they hear?
15. What appeared in the sky?
16. What did the people think was going to happen?
17. What did the seagulls do when they landed?
18. How were the people saved?
19. What is the name of the city which grew from the village?
20. Who often draw pictures of crickets and seagulls?

QUESTIONS ON THE INTERESTING FACTS.

1. (a) Where are ducks to be seen?
   (b) What kind of bills have they?
2. (a) How would you know geese in flight?
   (b) What kind of feet have they?
3. (a) Where are swans to be seen?
   (b) What sounds do they make when angry?
4. (a) Where do herons live?
   (b) How do they catch fish?
5. (a) Describe gulls in flight.
   (b) Where do they often rest?
6. (a) Why are terns called "Sea swallows"?
   (b) What sounds do they make?
7. (a) What do puffins look like?
   (b) Where do they nest?
8. (a) Gannets are very like_____only bigger.
   (b) How do they catch fish?

9. (a) Where are cormorants to be seen?
   (b) How would you know them in flight?
10. (a) Where do penguins live?
    (b) They are expert swimmers but cannot_____.

DEVELOPMENT EXERCISES

1. The story tells of an *army* of insects and a *flock* of seagulls. What is the name for a number of—cows, sheep, bees, puppies, wolves?
2. The brave little company crossed the country in big covered waggons. Nowadays we can travel much more easily and quickly. Name three ways by which you can go in comfort from one place to another.
3. The lake was called *Salt Lake*.
   (a) Is there anything strange about this name?
   (b) Why do you think it was so called?
   (c) Which of the following have salt water—bay, stream, sea, river, ocean, waterfall?
4. A seagull is a bird which lives by the sea.
   How do you think these birds got their names—wagtail, skylark, woodpecker, blackbird, cuckoo?
5. The people built huts and cabins.
   (a) Why did they make these little houses?
   (b) Where do you think they got the material to build?
   (c) Name and describe three other kinds of houses.
6. Where do sea birds usually make their nests?
   Name a bird which nests (a) on the ground, (b) in trees or bushes, (c) on high mountains.
7. Crickets are insects.
   (a) Name three crawling insects.
   (b) Name three flying insects.
8. The seagull is a swift graceful bird.
   Name birds which are (a) very fast fliers, (b) able to fly only a short distance, (c) unable to fly.

SAINT DAVID OF WALES

SAINT DAVID is the patron saint of Wales and the first of March is Saint David's Day. Many stories about his wonderful life have been handed down to us from long ago.

Although people knew him as Dewi Sant, he was baptised David, and it was at his baptism that his strange power was first shown. The monk, who held the baby boy, was blind. After David had been dipped in a spring, the monk sprinkled his own eyes three times with the same water, and then the miracle happened—he was able to see.

When David was a boy, he was taught by a clever man called Paulinus. As a result of his good and wise teaching, the lad grew up to be a noble and upright priest. David gathered about him a number of monks and they built churches in many parts of England. He felt however, that he should bring the gospel to his own country, and so he returned to Wales.

One day, David and his monks went to a place called Vallis Rosina, where they made a huge fire. The smoke from the flames rose high into the air and could be seen for miles around.

"Do you see that smoke?" said Boia, a chief who stayed nearby. "The man, who set that fire alight, will be the greatest man in the country."

"Go and kill him!" replied his wife, who was very angry. She did not wish anyone to become more powerful than her husband.

The chief gave orders to some of his soldiers, and a little later he led them towards the fire. On the way, Boia and his men were overcome by illness, and they were forced to return without doing any harm to David and his monks.

When they reached home, they were met by Boia's wife. "A terrible thing has happened!" she cried. "All our sheep and cattle have died while you were away!"

Boia and his wife were filled with fear and sorrow, and both went to see David. "Forgive us and have mercy upon us!" they said. "Restore our animals to life, so that our people can live, and we will give you the land of Vallis Rosina for ever." When the chief and his wife returned, they found that all their animals were alive and healthy.

David built a monastery at Vallis Rosina. His monks pulled the ploughs in order to till the soil. To provide honey they kept bees. When the outdoor work was over, the monks spent the rest of the day in study and prayer.

One day, the monk, who looked after the bees, set out on a journey to Ireland. A great swarm of the insects followed him to the ship and refused to leave him. The monk took them back to the monastery, but they followed him again when he left. Once more he returned to the monastery. At the third time David said to the monk: " Take them with you. They will prosper in the new land." Since then Ireland has been rich in bees and honey.

David made a journey to Jerusalem, and had many exciting adventures on his way to and from the Holy City. When he returned to Wales, great crowds flocked to hear him preach. He caused many churches and monasteries to be built in Wales, and he became the most famous bishop in the land.

At last Saint David's long life drew to an end and he was buried in his own monastery. For hundreds of years after his death, pilgrims came from far and near to visit his tomb and to honour this truly great man.

(Adapted)

QUESTIONS ON THE STORY.

1. What is the title of the story?
2. When is Saint David's Day?
3. By what name did people know him?
4. Tell the story of David's baptism.
5. What was the name of his good and wise teacher?
6. Where did David make a huge fire?
7. Who saw the smoke?
8. What did he say?
9. What did his wife tell him to do?
10. What happened to the chief and his soldiers?
11. What happened at home while they were away?
12. Who went to see David?
13. What did they say to him?
14. What did they find on their return?
15. Where did David build his first Welsh monastery?
16. How did the monks till the soil?
17. What did they keep to provide honey?
18. Tell the story of the monk and the bees.
19. To which far-off place did David make a pilgrimage?
20. Who came to honour him after his death?

LONE DOG

I'M a lean dog, a keen dog, a wild dog, and lone ;
I'm a rough dog, a tough dog, hunting on my own ;
I'm a bad dog, a mad dog, teasing silly sheep ;
I love to sit and bay the moon, to keep fat souls from sleep.

I'll never be a lap dog, licking dirty feet,
A sleek dog, a meek dog, cringing for my meat,
Not for me the fireside, the well-filled plate,
But shut door, and sharp stone, and cuff, and kick, and hate.

Not for me the other dogs, running by my side,
Some have run a short while, but none of them would bide.
O mine is still the lone trail, the hard trail, the best,
Wide wind, and wild stars, and the hunger of the quest !

Irene R. McLeod

LEATHER

"*THERE'S nothing like leather.*" That is the boast of the shoemaker.

Have you ever wondered where leather comes from ... that tough, yet soft and hard-wearing stuff which has so many different uses?

Leather is skin with the hair, fur, or wool removed. Nowadays the skins of many different kinds of creatures such as the cow, horse, sheep, goat, pig, deer, buffalo, antelope, walrus, lizard, snake, crocodile, and even the shark, are used to make leather. The skins of the larger animals are called "hides," and those of the smaller animals are called "skins."

The first thing to be done is to remove the skin as carefully as possible, so that it comes off in one whole piece. The fleshy side of the skin is rubbed with salt, in order to prevent decay, and then it is sent on to a leather factory or tannery.

At the tannery, the skins are cut to remove all useless parts and thrown into large tanks of salted water called brine. Here they are left for two or three days to be softened and cleaned. When the skins are taken out, they are put into a machine which cuts away all remaining bits of flesh.

LEATHER

The skins are next placed in a tank containing lime, which loosens the hair, fur, or wool. From there they are placed in a machine, which easily scrapes off the hair, fur, or wool, and splits the skins into two sheets. The hair side is called " grain leather " and the flesh side is called " suède leather." The skins are now ready for tanning.

The purpose of tanning is to make the skins soft, yet tough, and proof against water. This is done by hanging them in tanks of water containing a brown dye, usually oak bark. The skins pass through several of these tanks, each one with a stronger mixture than the one before.

To make soft leathers such as kid, chamois, and buckskin, the tanning is done in oil and the surface rubbed with emery.

The skins are next dried, oiled, and ironed by large heavy rollers. At last we have fine sheets of leather which are sent to factories to be made into different kinds of things such as boots, shoes, jackets, chair-covers, purses, pouches, school-bags, hand-bags, luggage cases, gloves, horse-harness, bicycle-saddles, footballs, and dog-collars.

QUESTIONS ON THE STORY.

1. What is the boast of the shoemaker?
2. What is leather?
3. Which farm-yard animals give us leather?
4. Which wild animals give us leather?
5. Which reptiles give us leather?
6. Which fish gives us leather?
7. What are the skins of the larger animals called?
8. Why must the skin be taken off carefully?
9. With what is the fleshy side rubbed?
10. Why is this done?
11. What is another name for a leather factory?
12. Which stuff loosens the hair, fur, or wool?
13. Into how many sheets is each skin split?
14. What is " grain " leather?
15. What is "suède " leather?
16. What is the purpose of tanning?
17. How are soft leathers made?
18. Name two soft leathers.
19. How are hides dried and ironed?
20. Name six things made of leather.

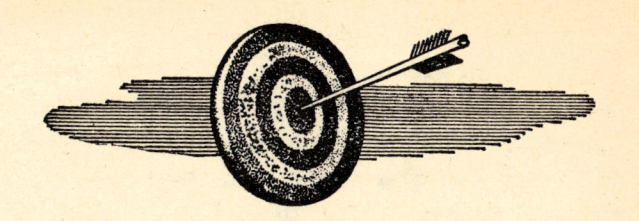

WILLIAM TELL

THE beautiful little country of Switzerland was once conquered by the Austrians, and the Swiss people were ruled by a very cruel and wicked Austrian named Gessler. He set up a high pole in the market-place of the village of Altdorf, placed an Austrian hat on the top, and ordered the Swiss people to bow to it as they passed by.

One day, William Tell, the finest archer in the country, came down from his home in the mountains to visit friends in Altdorf. With him was his only son, a boy of about ten years of age. They passed by the pole but did not bow. At once several soldiers caught hold of the father and took him before Gessler.

"Why did you not bow to the hat?" asked Gessler.

"I am a Swiss," replied Tell. "Why should I bow to an Austrian hat?"

"You will die if you don't!" said the wicked Gessler.

"I would rather die than bow to it," replied Tell.

"Take him away!" shouted Gessler to the soldiers. "We will deal with him later."

As Tell was being led away, Gessler changed his mind and ordered him to be brought back.

"I shall give you a chance," he said. "I hear that you are a famous archer. We will see if you are as good as people say you are. I will test your skill and this is what you must do. You will take your son and place an apple on his head. You will then stand forty paces away and shoot an arrow through the apple. If you do so, I shall spare your life. If you fail, you will be put to death."

"Kill me, if you wish," replied Tell, "but do not ask me to risk harming my son."

"You will do as I order!" shouted Gessler in anger. "If you don't, I'll put both you and your son to death."

The boy was then tied to a tree and an apple placed on his head. William Tell took an arrow, looked at it carefully, and slipped it under his belt. Then he took another arrow and fitted it to his bow.

WILLIAM TELL

The watching crowd was silent whilst he took aim. Ping! The arrow sped through the air, straight to its mark, and split the apple in two pieces. Not a hair of the boy's head was touched. The crowd cheered.

"A good shot!" cried Gessler. "But tell me, why did you put an arrow under your belt?"

"If my son had been hurt, the other arrow was for you."

The Austrian was furious, but, as he had promised to spare Tell's life, he could not kill him there and then. "Bind him with ropes!" he ordered. "Take him across the lake to the dungeon in my castle. That will teach him a lesson."

Tell was bound with ropes and taken to a boat, which was waiting on the shore. The soldiers threw the unhappy man into the bottom of the boat, and jeered at him. On their way across the lake, a great storm arose, and the soldiers set Tell free in order to help them.

He took the helm and steered the boat towards the rocks. When he reached them, Tell suddenly sprang ashore, and so escaped to the mountains he knew so well. The ship was wrecked and some of the soldiers were drowned.

Some days later, Gessler, who was searching in the mountains for Tell, passed the place where the famous archer was in hiding. When Tell saw him coming, he took an arrow from his belt, fitted it to his bow, and took careful aim. The arrow did not miss, and the wicked Gessler fell dead.

(Adapted)

WILLIAM TELL

Can you name them? By whom are they worn?

QUESTIONS ON THE STORY.

1. What is the title of the story?
2. In which country did the story take place?
3. Who conquered the Swiss people?
4. What was the wicked ruler's name?
5. Why did he place the hat on the top of the pole?
6. Who came to visit his friends?
7. What age was the boy?
8. Why did the soldiers arrest Tell?
9. What did Gessler order him to do?
10. How was the archer forced to do it?
11. What did Tell do with the first arrow?
12. What did he do with the second arrow?
13. How far was he from his son?
14. Why did the crowd cheer?
15. What did Gessler say to him?
16. What orders did he give to his soldiers?
17. What happened on their way across the lake?
18. Why did they free Tell in the boat?
19. How did he escape?
20. What happened to Gessler some days later?

DEVELOPMENT EXERCISES

1. The people of Switzerland are called the Swiss people.
   What are the peoples of the following countries called?
   England, Scotland, Ireland, Wales, France, Germany, Spain, Italy, Greece, Holland.
2. To what building should you go if you want to :—
   (a) catch a train? (b) buy a stamp? (c) buy petrol for a car? (d) save your money? (e) see a film?
3. Why do people
   (a) wear hats? (b) carry umbrellas? (c) wear shoes? (d) wash every day? (e) wear spectacles? (f) shake hands? (g) read newspapers? (h) eat food?

WILLIAM TELL

4. Gessler was a very wicked man.
   Why is it wrong to
   (a) steal? (b) tell lies? (c) throw stones? (d) be cruel to animals? (e) play on the street? (f) be greedy? (g) cheat at lessons or games? (h) be rude?

5. Under the following titles, write as many of each kind as you can. Hats_____ Footwear_____ Articles of Clothing.

6. Find the missing letters and then write out the words.
   (a) Worn on the foot   -oo-.   (f) Not shallow   -ee-.
   (b) A stupid person   -oo-.   (g) A rock in the sea   -oe-.
   (c) Shines at night   -oo-.   (h) To cry   -ee-.
   (d) What you eat   -oo-.   (i) The skin of an orange -ee-.
   (e) Middle of the day -oo-.   (j) A very swift animal -ee-.

7. All the following words contain " ough." See if you can say them correctly :— although, bough, cough, dough, enough, plough, rough, tough, though, through.

8. William Tell used a bow and arrow.
   Who use a (1) rifle, (2) tomahawk, (3) baton, (4) boomerang, (5) harpoon?

THE SCARECROW

A scarecrow stood in a field one day,
    Stuffed with straw, stuffed with hay,
He watched the folk on the king's highway,
    But never a word said he.

Much he saw but naught did heed,
    Knowing not night, knowing not day,
For having naught, did nothing need.
    And never a word said he.

A little grey mouse had made its nest,
    Oh so wee, Oh so grey,
In a sleeve of a coat that was poor Tom's best,
    But the scarecrow naught said he.

His hat was the home of a small jenny wren,
    Ever so sweet, ever so gay,
A squirrel had put by his fear of men,
    And hissed him, but naught heeded he.

Ragged old man, I loved him well,
    Stuffed with straw, stuffed with hay,
Many's the tale that he could tell,
    But never a word says he.

Michael Franklin.

A BRAVE BOY

HOLLAND is one of the world's greatest wonders as it is a country which is mostly below the level of the sea.

It is a very flat country with hardly a hill to be seen, and the people have built huge sand-dunes and dykes, to prevent the water from flooding the land. Even the little children were taught that the dykes must be watched every moment, and that the tiniest hole was dangerous.

Many years ago, there lived in Holland a little boy, whose name was Peter. One afternoon, his mother called him from his play. "Peter! I want you to go across the dyke to the cottage of our old friend Hans. Take these cakes I made for him. If you go quickly and do not stop to play, you should be home again before sunset."

The little boy was delighted to go on such an errand, and started off with a light heart. Twenty minutes later, he arrived at the old man's house. Peter was very fond of old Hans, because he told him so many interesting tales about the wonderful things he had seen in different parts of the world.

Hans was at home and very pleased to greet his young visitor. Nothing would do but he must tell a story. The old man told how, on one of his long voyages to the Far East, the moon darkened the sun in daytime. On the way back, there was a terrible earthquake and many people lost their lives.

Suddenly, Peter remembered his mother's wish that he return before dark and so, with a quick good-bye to his old friend, he set out for home. As he walked along, he gathered some flowers that grew beside the path, and he heard the angry waters dashing against the other side of the wall.

Listen! What was that? He heard the sound of trickling water, something quite different to the noise of the waves. He stopped and listened again. There must be a hole in the dyke somewhere, and he knew how very serious that could be.

Peter dropped his flowers, and searched carefully till he saw a tiny stream of water flowing from a small hole

A BRAVE BOY

in the dyke. What should he do ? It was a very lonely place, and he was afraid to go home for help, because the hole, if left, would quickly grow bigger. Peter knew the danger and how this leak could soon grow to be a flood.

Peter shouted, but no one answered. Suddenly, a thought came to him. Bending down, he pushed his hand as far as he could into the hole. This stopped the water, but it also meant that he must stay there till help came.

An hour went by, and although he watched along the dyke, no one passed. Again and again he shouted, but no one heard him. His hand and arm grew very stiff and cold, and he was lonely and tired, yet he would not leave his post.

During this time, his mother had been anxiously waiting for him, but when darkness came she closed and locked the cottage door, because she thought that Peter must be staying the night with old Hans. In the morning, when he returned, she would scold him for staying away from home without permission.

What was happening to poor Peter ?

The hours passed, and, in the darkness of the night, he scarcely knew what to do. He tried to whistle, but his teeth chattered with the cold. He thought of the family at home in their warm beds. " I must not let them be drowned " he said to himself, " even if I have to stay here all night."

The moon and stars looked down on the brave boy crouching against the dyke. His head was bent and his eyes were closed, but he was not asleep. Every now and again he would shout for help, but it was all in vain.

Early next morning a postman, who was going to his work, thought he heard a groan. There, by the side of the dyke, he saw a boy with his hand thrust into a hole in the wall. The man shouted to several men who were following behind him, and they ran to the boy's assistance.

Very tenderly, they lifted him up and rubbed his arm. Some of the men set to work at once to mend the dyke. Others carried the little hero home, as he was too weak even to walk.

Luckily, after a few days in bed, Peter was all right again. The people of the village were very proud of him, and they loved to tell the story of how little Peter saved the village.

INTERESTING FACTS ABOUT WONDERS OF NATURE.

1. **A Rainbow** appears as a round arch with bands of different colours. It is caused by the rays of the sun being bent while shining through falling raindrops.

2. **Volcanoes** are mountains with deep openings in the top. Sometimes they boil up inside, and throw out hot ashes, dust, steam, and melted rock called lava. The most famous volcanoes are Vesuvius, Etna, Stromboli, Hecla, and Cotopaxi.

3. **A Desert** is a bare sandy stretch of land, on which few creatures can live, and few plants can grow. The largest deserts are the Sahara, Gobi, Arabian, and Kalahari.

4. **Lightning** is a great flash of electricity in the sky. The **Thunder**, which follows it, is the sound of the air coming together after the passage of lightning.

5. **Icebergs** are huge mountains of ice which float in the cold seas near the North and South Poles. The part below the water is about eight times bigger than the part you see above the water.

WONDERS OF NATURE

6. A Geyser is a hot or boiling spring which spouts steam and water. Geysers are to be found in New Zealand, Iceland, and the United States.

7. Lakes are mostly stretches of fresh water. The Pitch Lake of Trinidad contains tar instead of water. In the Salt Lake of America and the Dead Sea the water is very salty.

8. The Aurora Borealis or Northern Lights is a strange yet beautiful sight. It is a huge arch of different colours from which streamers of light dart across the sky.

9. Earthquakes are shakings of the earth. They happen suddenly, and cause great damage and loss of life. Italy, India, China, Japan, New Zealand, and the west coast of America are troubled by them.

10. An Eclipse of the sun, means that the moon is passing between the earth and the sun. We can then see only that part of the sun which is not hidden by the moon. While this is happening, daylight fades.

A BRAVE BOY

QUESTIONS ON THE STORY.

1. What is the title of the story?
2. In which country did the story take place?
3. What kind of country is Holland?
4. What was the little boy's name?
5. Whom did he go to see?
6. What did he carry with him?
7. How long did the boy take on his journey?
8. What story did old Hans tell him?
9. Why did the boy leave his friend with a quick good-bye?
10. What did he do on his way home?
11. What caused him to stop and listen?
12. What did he find?
13. How did Peter stop the water?
14. What did his mother do when darkness came?
15. What did she think had happened to Peter?
16. The boy's hand and arm became _____
17. What did the postman hear on his way to work?
18. Who ran to the boy's help?
19. Some of the men set to work _____
20. Why did the others carry the little hero home?

QUESTIONS ON THE INTERESTING FACTS.

1. (a) Describe a rainbow.
   (b) How is it caused?
2. (a) What is a volcano?
   (b) Name three famous volcanoes.
3. (a) What is a desert?
   (b) Name two large deserts.
4. (a) What is lightning?
   (b) What is thunder?
5. (a) What are icebergs?
   (b) Where are icebergs to be seen?

6. (a) What is a geyser ?
   (b) Where are geysers to be found ?
7. (a) Name two strange kinds of lake.
   (b) What is strange about them ?
8. (a) Describe the Aurora Borealis.
   (b) What is it sometimes called ?
9. (a) What is an earthquake ?
   (b) Name any country which is troubled by them.
10. (a) What is an eclipse of the sun ?
    (b) What happens at the same time ?

DEVELOPMENT EXERCISES

1. From the following list, write out the words which should always begin with a capital letter.
   william, mother, holland, dyke, mary, cottage, world, monday, country, april, village, london.

2. To whom should you go if you want
   (a) a tooth taken out ? (b) your hair cut ? (c) your shoes mended ? (d) a bottle of medicine ? (e) to buy bread and cakes ?

3. Here are some curious creatures. Can you name them ?
   (a) A bird which can talk.
   (b) An animal which can travel for days without food.
   (c) A bird which lays its egg in another bird's nest.
   (d) An animal which carries its young in a pocket.
   (e) A bird which sings at night.
   (f) An animal which lives among the trees.
   (g) A bird which cannot fly.
   (h) An animal which can fly.

4. A **trickle** of water is a tiny stream of water.
   What is meant by a (1) shower, (2) storm, (3) downpour, (4) torrent, (5) flood ?

A BRAVE BOY

5. Peter's mother baked some cakes **in the oven**.
   Put the following in the sentences best suited to them :—
   in the basin, on the chair, in the cupboard, on the fire, on the floor, on the table, on the wall, on the mat.
   (1) I put some coal _____
   (2) I washed my hands _____
   (3) I sat _____
   (4) I wiped my feet _____
   (5) I hung the picture _____
   (6) I spread the tea-cloth _____
   (7) I laid the carpet _____
   (8) I put away the dishes _____

6. The postman wears a uniform while working. Name others who wear a uniform at their work.

7. A flat stretch of land is called a **Plain**.
   What name is given to
   (a) a piece of land surrounded by water ?
   (b) a stretch of water surrounded by land ?
   (c) the low ground between hills ?
   (d) a very high peak of land ?
   (e) a point of land stretching out into the sea ?

8. Peter put his hand into the **hole**.
   Write sentences using :—
   (a) mother____cakes____oven.
   (b) Hans____stories____world.
   (c) boy____pencil____desk.
   (d) girl____doll____floor.
   (e) lady____flowers____garden.
   (f) dog____cat____tree.

THE BROWN KING

In two more days it would be Tom's birthday. The cook of the Double-Diamond Ranch had promised to make a special cake, but best of all, Tom's father, who owned the great cattle ranch, had said that he would give him any horse he wished as a present. Tom had always wanted to be a cowboy, and a cowboy must have a good horse.

The boy thought of the horse he desired more than all others, a big brown stallion who was the leader of a great herd of wild horses, which roamed the hills near the ranch. Never had he seen a horse so swift or beautiful, except perhaps the white mare, who followed close to him wherever he went. Truly *he* was the King of the herd, and *she* was the Queen.

Now, when Tom's father had said that he would give him any horse he wished as a present, he thought only of one of his own horses. He was surprised when Tom told him that he wanted the leader of the herd of wild horses, but he promised to do his best to capture him.

Soon after dawn next morning, Tom's father gathered his cowboys together, and told them of his plan to catch the Brown King. The rancher and his men mounted

THE BROWN KING

their horses and set off to find the herd. They had not gone far, when one of the party caught sight of the animals grazing in Clover Valley. By good luck, they were able to get quite close to them without being seen.

Tom's father gave a signal and, with a sudden rush, two of the cowboys rode into the herd, and made straight for the leader. Swish! swish! and two ropes were over the Brown King's head. When the proud horse felt the tug of the ropes round his neck, he plunged and kicked in anger. In vain he tried to get rid of the ropes and, after a desperate struggle, he was beaten. Tired and weary, the brave fighter was led to the ranch and put into the corral. Tom's birthday present had arrived.

Many times did Brown King try to escape from his prison, but the high fence, which had barbed wire on the top, was too much for him, and he had to admit defeat.

Later that day, when all was quiet and still ... who suddenly appeared outside the corral, but the Queen. On catching sight of his faithful mate, the King jumped and kicked in great excitement. One of the cowboys, who was resting in a bunkhouse, heard the noise and came out to see what was wrong. As soon as the Queen saw him, she made off towards the open prairie.

When Brown King saw that she was leaving him, he made one last desperate bid to escape. He ran swiftly across the corral and, with a tremendous jump, tried to clear the fence. Alas, his legs caught on the wire, and he fell heavily to the ground. The poor animal lay perfectly still, and the cowboy, who saw the accident, ran to the ranch-house for help.

THE BROWN KING

A few minutes later, Tom's father and some of the cowboys took the horse into the comfort and shelter of the stable. One of the men went for a doctor, and another ran to the house for hot water and bandages.

When Tom reached the stable, there were tears in his eyes as he bent over the injured horse. He gently patted the glossy coat, stroked the fine long mane, and whispered into the animal's ear. Brown King slowly turned his head towards the boy, and munched feebly at the lumps of sugar, which Tom offered on his hand.

About four hours later, the doctor arrived. He examined the horse very carefully, and said it was suffering from shock and deep cuts. He said too, that there were no bones broken, and that the animal would be better in a few days.

Early next morning, Tom went to see his injured friend. To his surprise, he saw White Queen standing quietly beside the stable door. Tom held out a few lumps of sugar on his hand, and she came forward slowly and took them. The boy then opened the stable door and entered, closely followed by the mare.

As soon as the King saw his Queen, he raised his head from the straw, and gave a low whinny of welcome. The mare pushed past Tom, and stooped to lick the bandaged legs, and rub her nose against his neck and head.

The boy went away, but he left the stable door open, so that the mare could leave whenever she wished. He returned to the house, and had just started to his breakfast, when he heard loud yells from outside. Rushing to the window he saw two men jump through the open door of a bunk-house, just in time to escape a savage bite from White Queen.

Tom's father and the cowboys were very worried when they heard about it. The stallion might starve to death, if the mare would not allow anyone to enter the stable. What was to be done?

Tom, who was listening to them, placed a handful of sugar lumps in his pocket, and slipped quietly outside. The boy went to the storehouse, filled a large bucket

THE BROWN KING

with corn, and carried it to the stable. As he entered, an angry snort greeted him, but a moment later, the mare was pushing her nose into his pocket, in the hope of finding the little white things which tasted so sweet. While she was doing this, the boy fed the injured stallion. When he had finished, Tom gave them both several lumps of sugar.

For the next few days, no one but Tom was allowed to enter the stable, and he alone looked after the feeding and cleaning of the two wild horses. The three became great friends, and the horses grew fonder and fonder of lumps of sugar.

Then the day came when Brown King was all right again. Tom went down to the stable, opened the door, and turned them both loose. They ran out and galloped away to the open prairie. With a sad heart, Tom watched them disappear in the distance. He had grown so fond of them that he could hardly bear to part with them.

32

That same evening, as the sun was setting, there was a sudden loud noise. A cowboy, his face all smiles, shouted to Tom to come at once. What he saw made him the happiest boy in the world. The two horses had returned. When they spied Tom, they rushed towards him and pushed their noses into his pockets. The boy joyfully patted their necks, and then led them to the stable.

Brown King and White Queen had found a home.

THE BROWN KING

INTERESTING FACTS ABOUT COWBOYS.

1. Cowboys are the men who look after cattle in the same way as shepherds look after sheep. They guard the herds against **rustlers** or cattle-thieves, and keep the cattle away from dangerous rocks and cliffs. They work very hard and lead an **open-air life**.

2. Cowboys work on large grass farms called **ranches**. Some ranches stretch for miles and miles and are too big to have fences round them. The owner's home is called the **ranch-house**, and near to it are the log-cabins or **bunk-houses** of the cowboys. The **corral** is a fenced-in piece of ground, in which animals, such as horses and cattle, can be kept.

3. Cowboys have to ride long distances in order to keep a good watch on their cattle. They are very fond of horses, and spend most of the day in the saddle. Very often, the cowboys capture and tame some of the wild horses, which roam about the country.

4. Every spring, the cowboys round up their cattle and brand the young calves. This is done by pressing a hot iron against the animal's skin. Each owner has his own special mark. Later in the year there is a beef round-up. All the animals, which are to go to the market, are gathered together, and then driven on foot to the towns where they are to be sold.

5. Cowboys wear clothes which are useful in their work.

- (a) A **Stetson** is a special kind of hat. It is thick, to keep out the hot rays of the sun, and has a high crown for coolness. This hat has also a thick wide brim, which does not flop about the ears or lose shape with a soaking.
- (b) The **neckerchief** is a silk scarf worn around the neck. It is cool on a hot day, and warm on a chilly night. It is also used to prevent dust getting into the mouth and nostrils, or as a sling for a hurt arm.
- (c) A thick, coloured, woollen **shirt** with large breast pockets is usually worn. Cowboys sometimes wear a short leather sleeveless jacket, not unlike an open waistcoat.

THE BROWN KING

(*d*) **Chaps** are wide skin trousers, sometimes with hair on the outsides. These trousers keep their legs dry, and protect them from thorn bushes. They use thick leather belts which **can hold bullets**.

(*e*) As they work mostly on horseback, cowboys wear high-heeled, tight-fitting **riding boots with spurs**.

(*f*) To protect their hands and wrists, they wear buckskin **gauntlet gloves**, which are hard-wearing, yet soft.

6. In the bad old days, cowboys had to carry **guns** to defend themselves. The rifle was carried under the arm, or in a long leather holder or **holster** fitted to the **saddle** on the horse. The **Colt** (a heavy revolver) was carried in a short open holster fixed to the belt. So also was the **Bowie knife**, which was a pointed dagger with sharp edges. Cowboys caught animals by means of a long rope with a noose. In North America it was called **a rope**; in Mexico a **lariat**; and in South America a **lasso**. The South American cowboys also used a **bolas**; two or three balls connected by a rope.

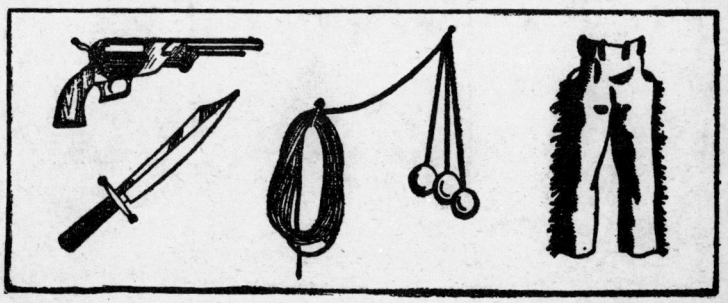

7. Cowboys are very good sports, and amuse themselves in a friendly way by trying to beat each other at roping, riding on bareback cattle and horses, and shooting at targets. Sometimes they go to a **rodeo** to win prizes at these sports. Cowboys are usually tall, keen of eye, bronze of skin, a little lean, but always very fit.

8. Cowboys are very fond of **music** and **singing**, and enjoy a sing-song round the camp fire. The mouth-organ, melodeon, fiddle, guitar, and banjo are the instruments they like best. They sing their **hill-billy songs** whenever they can, even to the cattle while riding with the herd.

9. In the days when many bad men such as murderers, rustlers, robbers, and outlaws roamed about the **Wild West**, it was very difficult to keep law and order. Sheriffs, deputies, state-marshals, Texas Rangers, and Mounted Police did their best to protect the people and, after a hard struggle, defeated those who tried to live by crime.

10. Besides cattle and horses, many other creatures live on the wide grass-lands and deserts.

(a) **Prairie dogs** or **gophers** are really large ground squirrels. They are pests and live in large numbers in underground towns.

(b) **Jack Rabbits** are a kind of hare.

(c) **Coyotes** are prairie wolves which have a habit of howling at night.

(d) **Big buzzards** are large vultures which eat dead flesh.

(e) **Rattlesnakes** are dangerous serpents, but give warning before they strike.

(f) **Lizards** are mostly harmless, but a great nuisance.

(g) **Tarantula spiders** are poisonous and dangerous.

QUESTIONS ON THE STORY.

1. What is the title of the story?
2. What was the name of the ranch?
3. What did Tom's father say he would give him?
4. What did the cook promise for his birthday?
5. What did Tom want to be when he grew up?
6. Which horse did Tom ask his father to get for him?
7. Where did this horse live?
8. Which animal was always with him?
9. Where did the cowboys first see the wild horses?
10. How were the hunters lucky?
11. How did the cowboys capture Brown King?
12. Where did they take him?
13. How was the horse injured?
14. What did the doctor say?
15. Who was standing by the stable door on the next day?
16. Why were Tom's father and the cowboys very worried?
17. Of what were the horses very fond?
18. What happened when Tom turned them loose?
19. Why was the boy so sad?
20. Describe the return of Brown King and White Queen.

QUESTIONS ON THE INTERESTING FACTS.

1. What is a cowboy's work?
2. (a) What is a large grass farm for cattle called?
   (b) Where did the cowboys live?
3. Why do cowboys need a horse?
4. (a) What is the main work of a cowboy in spring?
   (b) What is a beef round-up?
5. Describe a cowboy's
   (a) hat, (b) scarf, (c) shirt, (d) jacket, (e) trousers, (f) boots, (g) gloves.
6. What is a (1) holster, (2) Colt, (3) Bowie, (4) lariat?
7. Of what sports are cowboys fond?
8. (a) What musical instruments do they like best?
   (b) What name is given to their kind of songs?

THE BROWN KING

9. Who fought against the rustlers and robbers in the bad old days?
10. Name five creatures which live on the wide grass lands and deserts.

DEVELOPMENT EXERCISES

1. Brown King was a stallion and White Queen was a mare.
    Give the feminine of :—bull, cock, gander, lion, drake, tom-cat, ram, Billy-goat, boar, stag.
2. A horse lives in a stable.
    Which animals live in a (1) sty, (2) kennel, (3) burrow, (4) byre, (5) form?
3. (*a*) Cowboys look after cattle.
    Who looks after (1) sheep, (2) goats, (3) pigs or swine?
    (*b*) Cowboys work on a ranch.
    Where does each of the following work :—(1) barber, (2) miner, (3) sailor, (4) porter, (5) clown?
4. (*a*) Cowboys use a rope in their work.
    Who use (1) plough, (2) anvil, (3) saw, (4) ticket-punch, (5) spanner?
    (*b*) Cowboys work mostly on horseback.
    Name others who ride on horses.
5. Horses like lumps of sugar. Of what are these creatures very fond? (1) dog, (2) cat, (3) monkey, (4) mouse, (5) donkey.
6. The cowboys tamed wild horses. What other creatures have been tamed and trained to work for man?
7. Describe the clothes of :—(1) a Red Indian, (2) an Eskimo, (3) a Chinaman, (4) a desert Arab, (5) an Egyptian.
8. Place the following correctly in their sentences.
    On his head; Round his neck; On his feet; Round his waist; Under his arm.
    (*a*) ———————the cowboy wore a belt.
    (*b*) ———————he carried a gun.
    (*c*) ———————he had a Stetson.
    (*d*) ———————he wore high-heeled riding boots.
    (*e*) ———————he tied a scarf.

THE STOLEN CHILD

WHERE dips the rocky highland
    Of Sleuth Wood in the lake,
There lies a leafy island
Where flapping herons wake
The drowsy water-rats;
There we've hid our faery vats,
Full of berries
And of reddest stolen cherries.
Come away, O human child!
To the waters and the wild
With a faery, hand in hand,
For the world's more full of weeping than
    you can understand.

Where the wave of moonlight glosses
The dim grey sands with light,
Far off by furthest Rosses
We foot it all the night,
Weaving olden dances,
Mingling hands and mingling glances
Till the moon has taken flight;
To and fro we leap
And chase the frothy bubbles,
While the world is full of troubles
And is anxious in its sleep.
Come away, O human child!
To the waters and the wild
With a faery, hand in hand,
For the world's more full of weeping than
    you can understand.

THE STOLEN CHILD

Where the wandering water gushes
From the hills above Glen-Car,
In pools among the rushes
That scarce could bathe a star,
We seek for slumbering trout
And whispering in their ears
Give them unquiet dreams;
Leaning softly out
From ferns that drop their tears
Over the young streams.
Come away, O human child!
To the waters and the wild
With a faery, hand in hand,
For the world's more full of weeping than
    you can understand.

Away with us he's going,
The solemn-eyed:
He'll hear no more the lowing
Of the calves on the warm hillside
Or the kettle on the hob
Sing peace into his breast,
Or see the brown mice bob
Round and round the oatmeal-chest.
For he comes, the human child,
To the waters and the wild
With a faery, hand in hand,
From a world more full of weeping than
    he can understand.

W. B. Yeats

EMBLEMS OF OUR NEIGHBOURS

Here are four short stories to show how a plant came to be an emblem of a country.

The Leek of Wales

Saint David told King Arthur that his soldiers, when in battle, should wear something which would let them know those who were their friends. As leeks were plentiful and easy to get, each of the soldiers put one in his cap.

The Shamrock of Ireland

Saint Patrick, when preaching the gospel on his journeys, used a shamrock to show how three could be united into one, and yet remain three. Thus it became a sacred plant to the Irish people.

The Thistle of Scotland

Long ago, fierce warriors came to Scotland from over the sea, to raid and to plunder. These robbers landed near a Scottish camp, and they made ready to attack in the dark. They crept with bare feet, so that they would make no noise, but, when the pirates came near to the Scots, a strange thing happened. They tramped on prickly thistles, and of course yelled with pain. The Scots were warned of danger, and were able to win an easy victory.

EMBLEMS OF OUR NEIGHBOURS

The Rose of England

A long time ago, there lived in England, two very powerful noblemen. One had as his emblem a red rose, while the other had a white rose. Their families fought against each other for many years, in what was called the Wars of the Roses. In the end, the soldiers of the white rose won, and their leader became King of England. In this way, the rose became the royal emblem of that country.

The Isle of Man has a very strange symbol which resembles three bent legs. It was in ancient times the symbol of the sun and is called the Triskele. This device is also the badge of Sicily.

Some Other National Emblems

Belgium	*Azalea*	Italy	*Lily*
Denmark	*Anemone*	Netherlands	*Tulip*
France	*Fleur-de-Lis*	Russia	*Sunflower*
	or *Cockerel*	Spain	*Pomegranate*
Germany	*Cornflower*	Sweden	*Twinflower*
Greece	*Violet*	Switzerland	*Edelweiss*

Two Very Unusual Emblems

Poland	*The Bluebottle*	Barbados	*The Flying Fish*

DEVELOPMENT EXERCISES

In your atlas find the above countries
1. Name the capital of each?
2. How many people live in each?
3. What are the principal industries of each?
4. What name is given to the people living in each?

SAFETY FIRST

BILLY BROWN lived in a big town. He had no garden in which to play, so he spent most of his time in the street. Now Billy liked very much to hang on the back of any passing motor-lorry and steal a ride. No wonder people called him " Silly Billy."

One day, he saw a motor-lorry coming down the street and, as it passed him, he sprang on the back. Not long afterwards, he jumped off, but alas! he did not see a van coming close behind him.

The van-driver tried hard to stop his car in time, but it was too late. Billy was knocked down and, sad to say, his arm was broken. He suffered great pain, and had to be taken in an ambulance to hospital.

For many weeks Billy lay in bed, and felt very sorry that he had caused so much trouble. When his father and mother and friends visited him he would say

I've learned a lesson! No more rides on lorries for me.

SAFETY ALWAYS

MARY GREEN lived in a little village. There was a nice playing field not far from her home, but she liked better to play with her ball on the road. Very foolishly, she thought that she would come to no harm, as there was very little traffic in that quiet village.

One day, as Mary was bouncing her ball on the road, a motor car swung round a corner, and was almost upon her before she noticed it. A passer-by saw her danger, and ran to her aid.

Too late! Mary was knocked down and her leg was badly injured. When Mary's mother arrived soon afterwards, the driver took them both in his car to the nearest hospital, which was twelve miles away.

Mary suffered much pain, and was forced to spend many weeks in bed, as she was unable to walk. She, just like Billy, learned a lesson when it was too late. As she did not wish the same to happen to any of her friends, Mary would say to them :—

Look at me! Don't play on the road.

AN EASTERN PROVERB

He who knows and knows he knows,
    He is a wise man : seek him.
He who knows and knows not he knows,
    He is asleep : wake him.
He who knows not and knows he knows not,
    He is a child : teach him.
He who knows not and knows not he knows not,
    He is a fool : shun him !